UNDAUNTED

UNDAUNTED

by Matthew Sandusky

Rothco Press • Los Angeles, California

Published by
Rothco Press
8033 West Sunset Blvd., Ste. 1022 • West Hollywood, CA 90046

Cover design by Rob Cohen

Rothco Press is a division of Over Easy Media Inc.

ISBN: 978-1-941519-87-5

E-Book: ISBN: 978-1-941519-88-2

ACKNOWLEDGEMENTS:

First and foremost, I would like to thank my wife Kim for standing beside me throughout the ups and downs of my journey while showing me unconditional love. You have been my inspiration and motivation for continuing to improve myself, my knowledge and to move forward on my healing path. You are my rock and you have allowed me the opportunity to tackle this difficult challenge. For these reasons and many more I dedicate this book to you.

I also want to thank my wonderful children. All of you are special and I am blessed and a better man each day because I have each of you in my life. Thank you for always making me smile and teaching me the important lesson of never taking life too seriously. My hope is that one-day when you read this book that you will be half as proud of me as I am of each of you everyday of my life.

Chris Anderson and Jolie Logan are just two of the hundreds of wonderful advocates I have had the privilege to meet. I consider you both great friends and want to thank you for your support and for believing in the work and me I am doing to bring awareness to child sexual abuse.

June Saunders thank you for the countless hours you put into editing this book.

Jim Clemente, Thank you for the hours you spent discussing this project with me. You have been a teacher and an inspiration. Your work inspired me to take the step to write this book. I could not have completed this project without your help.

Lastly, I want to thank my supporters. You have supported the work I am doing through Peaceful Hearts. I read every email and letter of support and encouragement. This book happened because of your support. Thank you for believing in the work we all are doing.

FOREWORD:

I first met Matthew Sandusky long after I'd heard of him. Many months after I'd studied the Jerry Sandusky case and written a scathing rebuke of the Freeh Report that had erroneously concluded the case was one of "Stranger Danger" instead of a "nice guy" acquaintance offender. This fundamental error temporarily set the field of child sexual victimization back several decades and in the process tried to make people believe it was the culture of football that was to blame for Jerry Sandusky getting away with his crimes for decades. In fact it was Jerry Sandusky's skill at manipulating boys into compliant victimization that was the real culprit.

I finally met Matt after I heard him tell his powerful and disturbing life story. A story that few people bothered to learn about before they condemned him for reversing his position and speaking out. It was as if some people blamed him for being a typical child sex crimes victim who never wanted anyone to know the indignities he'd suffered at the hands of his adoptive father, Jerry Sandusky. The truth however, is that Matt Sandusky overcame nearly insurmountable obstacles to make his heroic disclosure.

Some people claim he is lying. Some claim he did it for the money. But in these pages you will find the details that will help you understand the truth. A truth that is not nearly as clean and clear-cut as people would like it to be. It is messy and horrifying but very real. It is a truth of whispers and secrets and shame. A truth that far too many of us have endured for far too many decades. The truth is that Matt emerged as a pivotal and unwavering voice in a sea of disbelief, discontent, over-reaction and misunderstanding that overtook "Happy Valley" in the midst of a scandal of earth-shattering proportions.

The Jerry Sandusky case is a classic example of an effective grooming strategy executed by a "nice guy" "pillar of the community" acquaintance offender, leading to public adulation and compliant victimization of many boys for decades, and ultimately, years later, incremental disclosure by the men he sexually victimized as children.

What follows on these pages is not only an insightful and courageous disclosure, it is the most comprehensive proof of Jerry Sandusky's guilt and of the critical need to understand, recognize and root-out "nice guy" acquaintance offenders set in the most contentious and misunderstood child sex crimes case of our time.

Read the words Matt has written carefully, for they reveal a truth that exposes the silent but putrid underbelly of victimization that continues to occur across this country and around this world, not by "stranger danger" or "monster predators," but by those we admire, trust and love. If you pay attention, you might just be part of the groundswell that is capable of protecting the children of your community from it rather than the "conspiracy of silence" that helps it fester and propagate in the darkness.

The Jerry Sandusky case ultimately had very little to do with football and everything to do with the fact that the most common and insidious danger to our children comes from those we willingly hand our children over to because we trust them.

In this book Matt explains in great detail why and how he maintained his silence for so long. He explains why he finally decided to open the floodgates and tell the truth about Jerry Sandusky. He brings the reader inside the careful manipulations and strategies implemented by Jerry Sandusky. And he finally and definitively answers the question: Did Jerry Sandusky really molest all of those boys?

Jim Clemente,
Retired FBI Supervisory
Special Agent/Profiler
& Survivor of Childhood
Sexual Victimization.

CHAPTER ONE:

The Biggest Scandal in College Football History

My name is Matthew Sandusky. No doubt you recognize the last name. "Jerry" Sandusky was one of the most admired and well-known assistant college football coaches in the United States. His fabulous reputation went down in flames as he was engulfed in the biggest scandal in college football history. Jerry Sandusky is in prison today, serving a life sentence for sexually abusing young boys over a period of two decades. He was convicted on 45 out of 48 counts relating to child molestation.

Jerry Sandusky was my foster father. Then I became one of his six adopted children.

After the last game he coached before his retirement, Jerry was carried off the field on the shoulders of his jubilant players. This 1999 contest was Pennsylvania State University versus Texas A & M at the Alamo Bowl in San Antonio. Jerry's outstanding defensive coaching was credited for the win; at least there seemed to be no doubt about that in the minds of his triumphant players. Before they buoyed him off the field, he received the ceremonial ice water dousing from them in recognition of his role in bringing about the win. Usually only head coaches receive this jubilant honor.

"THE DEAN OF LINEBACKER U"

Jerry was very good at his job, and he was loved for it. He was Pennsylvania State University's defensive line coach from 1969-1970, when he became the linebacker coach. He was so proficient at this, he was nicknamed the "Dean of Linebacker U." He raised up ten All-Americans and contributed a number of linebackers to the NFL. He was the Lions' defensive coordinator from 1977-1999, his career ending with his celebrated retirement. He wrote manuals and created videos on linebacker drills, fundamental principles for linebackers, defensive strategies, coaching and developing linebackers the Penn State way, and youth football.

When the scandal broke, people simply could not believe that the allegations of child sexual victimization were true about the spectacularly successful assistant coach. The Pennsylvania State Nittany Lions are a triumphant football team. The Lions have won two national championships (1982; 1986). They are part of the Big Ten Conference, and they have taken three Big Ten Conference Championships (1994; 2005; 2008) and have played at forty-five college bowl games. Their head coach, Joe Paterno, who was on the job from 1966 until 2011, was a legend in his own time. His photo appeared on the cover of *Sports Illustrated*, and he had over 400 wins to his credit (the highest in the history of the NCAA's Division 1 Football Bowl Subdivision). He was inducted into the College Football Hall of Fame.

Jerry Sandusky was part of most of those victories for Penn State. At a school and in a town that all but worshiped football, Jerry, too, was a living legend. He was admired and loved wherever he went in "Happy Valley" and was the heir apparent to Joe Paterno's football legacy.

JERRY'S NAME WAS LIKE GOLD IN HAPPY VALLEY

"Happy Valley" is the nickname for Pennsylvania State University and its environs, which include imposing Mount Nittany. The mountain overlooks and lends even more beautiful scenery to a town and campus that some have compared to Eden. Not far from its bucolic roots, the university has a herd of several hundred dairy cows, which supply cream for Berkey Creamery, a popular ice cream hotspot. A mixture of country authenticity and university chic make Penn State and it surroundings paradisial.

The grounds of the Penn State campus are verdant and abundant. The playing fields are meticulously cared for, as are the grand buildings. There are fashionable, tiny stores along the main street of the campus. There are 45,000 students at the University Park main campus, and 40,000 more students at branches of the university around the state. The school's budget is more than $4 million per year.

Penn State is considered one of the "public ivies," a publicly-funded university that is comparable in excellence to the Ivy League universities. For all intents and purposes, Penn State truly lives up to its "Happy Valley" moniker as a beautiful, cared for place of success of which citizens, faculty, and students are justly proud.

Much of that civic pride comes from the university's illustrious football program. "Happy Valley" speaks football—to the exclusion of nearly every other language! There was a seven-foot high statue of Joe Paterno on the grounds of Penn State, he was so admired and venerated. (The statue has since been taken down because of the scandal surrounding Jerry Sandusky and Joe's purported role in it.) As the assistant football coach, Jerry was only slightly less iconic than Joe Paterno in stature. These men were larger than life in Happy Valley.

I can tell you that, as Joe Paterno's right hand man, Jerry Sandusky's name was like gold. It could take you anywhere in that community. Also, he was a professor of physical education at Penn State and was granted emeritus status upon his retirement, which gave him many rights and privileges, including free parking and limitless access to the university's athletic facilities. Doors opened everywhere in front of Jerry Sandusky, and if he had adopted you as one of his "boys," you too seemed to have a pass to every gateway to joy in Happy Valley.

I was not formally adopted into the Sandusky family until I was eighteen, and the reasons for that were more practical than emotional, but I was like a member of his family long before that. It was known far and wide that Jerry favored me a great deal, and anywhere I went with him, gateways magically opened;

permissions were granted; rules were bent or broken for good ole' Jerry.

That he had a "heart of gold" was the most common perception of Jerry in Happy Valley, especially after he founded The Second Mile, a program for underprivileged youth, in the late seventies. The community thought he could do no wrong. His youth charity only added to the shining patina of his halo in the community's eyes. He was awe-inspiring. I have said that the perpetrator in my case was treated literally as though he was a god. Or let me amend that: Joe Paterno, it seemed to me, was treated as God and Jerry Sandusky was treated as his only begotten son.

I want to take a moment to discuss why I say "the perpetrator in my case" instead of always naming him or saying "my perpetrator." It is well documented that Jerry Sandusky is the person who sexually abused me from a very young age. He is the person who committed these crimes against me and therefore is not worthy of being related to me in any way. I have in the past referred to him as "my perpetrator" but have come to realize that by saying that, I was holding onto and keeping us forever linked together. As you read through the rest of this book, please know that I may not always refer to him by name but when I say "the perpetrator in my case" I am referring to Jerry Sandusky.

Jerry's father had been involved in youth work too, and the two of them were awarded a mutual Human Rights Award by the NAACP in 1993. In 1995 the YMCA gave Jerry an award for his service to youth. He received numerous other awards, including ones related to his charity foundation The Second Mile, which existed to serve underprivileged youth. Then, in 2011, investigators had come to the terrible conclusion that Jerry's charity work in The Second Mile had provided him with unusual access to children. It was speculated that perhaps he had even designed the program for the purpose of finding victims.

Gerald Arthur "Jerry" Sandusky was convicted of 45 counts of child victimization. Let me take a moment to describe exactly what that term means.

It is common to find multiple definitions of the terms related to Child Sex Crimes. At the FBI's National Center for the Analysis of Violent Crime, they use the term child sexual "abuse" to describe sexual victimization of a child within the family or within the ring of care and custody. Therefore, Jerry victimizing a foster or adopted child, i.e. myself, would be considered child sexual abuse, whereas Jerry victimizing a boy from The Second Mile would be considered sexual victimization. They like using the term Child Sexual Victimization (CSV) because it is an umbrella term that covers all forms of sexual crimes against children, while the term "abuse" covers intra-familial sexual crimes, and it also covers physical and emotional abuse of children. In other words, "Child Abuse" is a term people tend to use because it allows them to not have to say "sexual" victimization. Part of my mission is to make the "sexual" victimization of children a household topic so that we can finally start to eradicate it by bringing it out into clarity and the light.

Of course, not everyone believed Jerry was guilty. The disbelief and anger in Happy Valley over the allegations and convictions were widespread, and his accusers caught a lot of flak. What's more, the case against him (including the arrest) was delayed and delayed due in part to the fact that Jerry was so big, so iconic, and Penn State was so powerful and prestigious, prosecutors had to make sure they had a rock solid case against him before they dared to proceed. In fact some of the allegations of child sexual victimization dated back to 1998, yet Jerry was not arrested until November 6, 2011.

A HIGH STAKES CASE

Jerry was so well-respected, it was thought that his arrest might even affect high stakes elections and thus it may have been delayed by government officials. At the same time, there are quite a few instances in which it took a great deal of time to build a sufficient case to take down a "pillar of the community" offender. Some very high profile cases were not successful despite the decades of rumors of victimization and pay-offs to victims' families. These longer-term investigations are necessary because 1. They are private crimes, 2. No one can believe that the nice guy could be an offender, and 3. The common refusal on the part of victims to come forward. If they had arrested Jerry on the word of Victim #1 alone, Jerry would have crushed him at trial. He would have been eviscerated and re-victimized. The only thing I can really fault them with is not preventing Jerry from having access to boys during the pendency of the investigation, although it was speculated that the former attorney general, Tom Corbett, did not want to have Jerry arrested and have the fall-out of all that going on while he was running for governor.[1] Votes and donations could have been affected. There is no doubt that Jerry Sandusky had that kind of clout and appeal among Penn State related donors and certainly among The Second Mile's stellar board of directors and supporters. If Corbett was perceived as "going after" one of the superstars of Happy Valley, he might very well have faced electoral fall-out. However, the difficulty of bringing "pillar of the community" types down must be taken into account too.

Jerry had so much power in Happy Valley, that even after his arrest he and his attorney, Joe Amendola, were pretty confident they could sway the jury in his favor, even if he was being accused of nearly fifty counts of child endangerment, molestation, and rape.

That is, they were confident until I, Jerry's adopted son, made the difficult decision to disclose that Jerry had sexually victimized me and to testify against him if necessary.

THE CASE PIVOTS ON ME

My volunteering to testify against Jerry, as one of the boys he victimized and as one bearing his name as his legally adopted son, turned the trial on its ear. Jerry was going to testify on his

---

1 Sylvia L. Kurtz, *To Believe a Child: Understanding the Jerry Sandusky Case and Child Sexual Victimization* (Xlibris, 2014) p. 14.

own behalf, and the man had appeal. He had prestige. The man had power and charisma. His status as a community benefactor was huge, in addition to being a winning coach for the sainted football team. He never stopped maintaining his innocence, either, which sometimes sways people's opinions. Yet the way the justice system works, if Jerry took the stand, I had a right to take the stand as a rebuttal witness, and I was ready at last to reveal in a public forum what had been my private hell.

At that point, his attorneys decided that Jerry could not take the stand himself. "To put Jerry on the stand and have Matt come in and testify against him, it would destroy any chance of an acquittal," Joe Amendola, Jerry's lawyer, told reporters.

Thus the self-excusing, steeped-in-denial, winning, and much-admired assistant football coach and public benefactor of Happy Valley would not be able to persuade the jury of his innocence from the witness stand. If he attempted to, my follow-up testimony would ruin any possibility he would have of being found innocent. Without necessarily meaning to, my coming forward at the time I did checkmated Jerry's legal defense.

It pivoted the case and helped lead to Jerry's convictions and sentencing of thirty to sixty years in prison. Since he was sixty-eight at the time of his conviction, that would essentially amount to a life sentence.

Thank goodness, that stopped the victimization of children by Jerry Sandusky for good. It had gone on for more than two decades (perhaps three or four). Although there had been hints as to his activities, Jerry was too slick and untouchable for all the filtering-in rumors to take hold. There had been incidents and reports about Jerry's inappropriate behavior with male children in shower rooms on campus dating back to 1998, but it took thirteen years to bring Jerry to justice.

I certainly believe I had a role in helping to bring his convictions about (and thus stopping the victimization). That is a good thing, although there have been times when I thought, if I had it to do over again, I might not disclose Jerry's victimization of me in order to spare my family what we went through after my story became public. However, the fact that Jerry was stopped, and that I was one of the bottlenecks in the continued flow of his victimization, makes me realize how important it was for me to speak out, even though it was a great sacrifice for me and my family to do so.

Not everyone welcomed my honesty, of course. As I mentioned, disbelief about the allegations against Jerry was widespread, and people did not hesitate to express how angry they were at all this. Denial was rampant in Happy Valley. In spite of the overwhelming evidence, some people lined up on Jerry's side, righteously indignant on his behalf. Some of these people were furious at me for my role in turning the trial on its ear. They said that all of Jerry's accusers, including me, were outright lying.

JoePa and Penn State

The scandal took on whole new dimensions in 2011 when it led to the summary firing of Joe Paterno, the most famous coach in college football. The university let the beloved Joe Paterno go because he had barely cleared the bar of his minimal legal responsibility to report allegations of child sexual victimization on campus when Mike McQueary told him of the shower horror in 2001. The scandal, already big and growing bigger due to Jerry's arrest and trial, became national and international news, with sports pundits and newscasters alike taking on the subject on all the major networks. The question became how much Joe knew and what he was morally responsible to have done about it.

Happy Valley itself went crazy when Joe Paterno was fired. There certainly did not seem to be much doubt in the eyes of its citizens that Joe hadn't done anything wrong and that he didn't deserve to have an illustrious career ended in this ignominious way. Thousands of students poured into the streets of downtown State College and on campus to protest the firing. They were blowing horns and shouting how much they wanted Joe Paterno back. In fact, there were demonstrations that turned into riots, property damage, and an overturned media vehicle that brought out cops in riot gear wielding pepper spray.

"We are Penn State!" they thundered on Joe Paterno's lawn, supporting him, and Joe Paterno spoke to them and pumped his fist in acknowledgment of their support. Penn State's football program under Joe Paterno was so beloved, that students camped out overnight in tents to be in line for the best tickets. Football was almost an obsession.

I'm happy to report that far more students, some ten thousand, turned out a few nights later outside of Penn State's Old Main administration building to hold a candlelight vigil for victims of child sexual victimization, including Jerry's victims. After all, while an injustice might have been done to Joe Paterno, victims of child sexual victimization suffer far greater injustices, and anyone in a position to help them should do their utmost to come to their aid. Victims of child sex crimes have their lives severely compromised by the victimization early on. From a young age, their lives are burdened by the trauma of early sexualization and violation of trust. It seems to me that the rights of children who are sexually victimized or who may be sexually victimized should come first—and responsible adults need to make sure those rights are treated with the utmost priority. Children who have suffered sexual victimization or those who may suffer it deserve the bulk of our indignation over any injustices, not the icons of any kind of sport.

However, for reasons I will go into, I understand why Joe Paterno didn't do more, and the reasons are understandable to people who are knowledgeable about the nature of child sexual victimization and child sexual offenders.

At the time, the statue of Joe Paterno on campus was taken down, along with its now seemingly ironic legend: "They ask me what I'd like written about me when I'm gone. I hope they write I made Penn State a better place, not just that I was a good football coach." His hopes were not to be fulfilled completely, although he is remembered with respect for his character-building in young men (and young women) as well as his achievements in football. At this point too, a Quinnipiac poll showed that almost 60% of Pennsylvanians polled, as opposed to 25%, favored the return of his statue to a prominent place on the campus. Pennsylvanians are also happy that the NCAA restored Joe Paterno's wins to return him to the top slot of the Division I's head coach winning list in 2015. His wins from 1998 to 2011 (the years from the first report of sexual victimization of children by Jerry Sandusky and the date of his arrest) had been temporarily taken away from him, relegating him to twelfth on the list of big coach winners rather than first. Those wins were restored.

Jim Clemente, retired FBI agent, an expert on child sexual victimization, maintains that Joe Paterno did not know enough to do anything about Jerry, and when he knew something, that something was very unclear. Because of this, Jerry continued to hang around a lot, using the shower rooms and the pool, and the locker rooms. This was part of Jerry's retirement package, and the privileges were never revoked, due to in part to the fact that Jerry was never charged with any crime and the only time someone thought they witnessed something, it was very unclear as to what they had witnessed exactly.

I know from my own experiences with Jerry that the Penn State locker rooms had a coded security system where you had to punch in numbers before entering, and there was plenty of warning time to hide what you were doing before anyone came in. Jerry loved to wrestle with his child victims in the locker room. I know because he had me pinned down there more than once. He had plenty of time, due to the coded security system, to assume more innocent "wrestling" postures with his victims when anyone else entered the locked room. At one point he even asked an adult who entered to count down a pin hold for him on me, and the adult complied, seeing it all as innocent, or at least not suspecting enough to report anything. The victimization went on.

This is all part of the brilliance of Jerry's grooming techniques and strategies. His innocent air and justification of his actions as being just fun with the kids not only "proved" to adults that what Jerry was doing was innocent, but it "PROVED" to the child that the child was helpless and that Jerry was bulletproof, and that no one would do anything to stop Jerry's sexual assaults. Everyone's silence, then, was reinforced.

Joe Paterno died of unrelated causes soon after his job was terminated. Although the matter bothered him a great deal, he was eighty-five years old and had undiagnosed lung cancer and a broken hip, all of which contributed to his death.

As mentioned, some of the honors stripped from him in response to the scandal have been restored. The man was still beloved by many after a spectacularly successful career in his chosen field. He had a loving a marriage that lasted all of his adult life, and a happy, supportive family. His was a life well lived and amply rewarded.

I understand the outrage felt by some of the victims, myself included, about the fact that some students and football fans seemed more incensed about Joe Paterno being fired than they were about Jerry molesting boys for decades. However, in Joe's and Penn Sate's defense, it is not as if Jerry's crimes were so open and notorious or he was such a visibly heinous "monster predator" that everyone who was close to him must have or should have been aware of the sexual victimization he was committing, including his bosses at Penn State. The truth is, Jerry was such a masterful and successful "groomer" of his victims and the community that those closest to him could not see him as anything other than a "saint" and a child advocate. Without a real understanding of "Nice Guy" offenders, people truly believe you have to be a thoroughly "bad" person to sexually assault children. Many people, including myself, know that is not true. In fact, the vast majority of children are victimized by someone they know, trust, and love- a nice guy, like Jerry Sandusky.

Nor do I believe that "the culture of football" was to blame. I believe it was Jerry Sandusky's grooming of his victims into compliant victimization and his grooming of the community into believing he was a saint who was incapable of doing anything harmful to children that caused all the blindness. If we lay the responsibility on football and the desire to protect that program, then we take focus away from the reality that sexual predators do not stand out to the people around them. Offenders in fact sometimes seem like godsends, like heroes. I know this from my own experience.

If we perpetuate this "football program as patsy" myth, we allow people to say to themselves, "Well, we have no football culture problem here in this town, so we don't have to scrutinize the nice guys who are hanging around our children." Thus we prevent people from actually examining the people in their lives that they trust and love and willingly turn their children over to, who are actually the real threat to their kids.

I believe it is important to understand that in pretty much every community, school, team, organization that deals with kids, there is the risk of nice guy acquaintance offenders infiltrating their ranks. The kinder and more tuned in to children they are, the less likely anyone will ever suspect that their motives for being around children are sexual. Jerry certainly had everyone convinced beyond a shadow of a doubt that he was a wonderful person who only had the best interests of children in his heart.

It is said that Joe Paterno did not think Penn State handled his report of the victimization very well: "If Jerry did what they say he did, then I think we all wish we had done more." Of course, Penn State had a responsibility to keep children safe and protected while on their property. Just like any other school, a youth-serving organization or church has the responsibility to protect children while on their premises. In theory, the possibility exists that someone in the administration suspected Jerry but was unconvinced that he was molesting boys so he did nothing about it. But unless and until that person gets his day in court, I believe it is wise to give him the presumption of innocence. Everyone knows from the example of the Catholic Church priest-child sex scandal that they did in fact vote to protect the reputation of the church over the safety of the child victims. There is always a possibility of that happening in any organization. Yet I am not aware of any proof of it in this case.

Up to his last months on this earth, Paterno could not bring himself to believe that Jerry was capable of molesting or sodomizing boys. Maybe it was willful denial, but I believe that, as in the hundreds of cases like this that I have studied, the people closest to the manipulations of an effective groomer are the ones who fall for it the hardest. Sure, in hindsight, all the red flags were there. But Paterno was not trained to recognize them and he was not an investigator. He was adverse to even speaking about sex. He was old school, advanced in years, and prudish about sex. His mind likely did not go to "anal sex" when McQueary told him he saw Jerry in the shower with a boy and that it was way over the line. Implication is not necessarily a completed communication. Paterno seems by all accounts to have been a man who actually cared deeply about his students, but, of course, his students were all adults. Paterno did not have a lick of experience working with kids, and he had no idea how nice guy, acquaintance offenders operate, grooming kids and the community.

To sum up, Jerry alone is responsible for Jerry's actions. Sometimes those closest to the abuser are the most convinced of his innocence as they see his community saintliness up close. It is sometimes just too hard to believe that something so opposite to that is taking place when he gets a child behind closed doors.

There are many different opinions as to whether Joe Paterno's actions, or the lack of them, as well as whether the actions or lack of them on the part of the Penn State administrators above him were justified or not. The argument can be made that Joe Paterno was in a position to stop young kids from being sexually victimized and he did the bare minimum of what he was legally

required to do, ignoring what he might have been morally required to do.

I believe it is possible that Joe Paterno, among many others,
might have done more to step in and prevent Jerry Sandusky
from molesting so many victims had they had the knowledge to
understand child sexual victimization and how nice guy offenders operate. I believe that the biggest scandal in college football
history had very little to do with college football or the people
involved in it. It had to do with Jerry Sandusky and the nature of
"nice guy" sexual offenders. In this, Jerry was a textbook case,
but he was a textbook case in a course very few people have tak-
en or understand.

CHAPTER TWO:

Speaking Truth to Power

Eventually it was voices of the little people, the disempowered, speaking truth to power that brought down Jerry Sandusky. It was single mothers speaking up on behalf of their fatherless children. It was the voices of the children crying out from their now adult bodies, that so effectively refuted Jerry's claims of innocence, penetrated the veil of his saintly image, and made sure that he was convicted. It was the voices of the victims disclosing their victimization, speaking truth to power that made power bow.

It took a long time, however, for the victims to find their voices. There are well-documented reasons for this. Victims of child sexual victimization almost never disclose the abuse. Sometimes people think that, because the victims never spoke up, that is proof that the abuse never took place. In fact, experts in the field of child sexual victimization see their silence as a factor that corroborates the truth of what victims finally reveal. Shame, guilt, and fear of stigma are all factors seen in real victimization survivors. Almost all of them are hesitant to speak up. We will go into more detail about this in a later chapter.

THE VERACITY OF THE VICTIMS

All the victims' stories tallied. The victims did not know one another well, nor did they consult with one another before testifying, but the stories are all chillingly the same. They tell of the singling out, the favoritism, the special attention, the grooming, the gifts and privileges, and the deep silence of the child victims as the victimization went on and on.

Jerry liked to give his favorites tickets to football games, introductions to the Lions in their locker room, athletic gear, computers, video games, and lots of personal attention. It made kids who had little going for them feel "cool," as several of the young men testified.

"He made me feel like I was part of something, like a family," said Victim Number 3. "He gave me things that I had never had before. I just didn't want to give any of it up." He said he loved Sandusky, who also proclaimed "that he loved me, that I was unconditionally loved, like a family." That kind of love was not available in the families of origin for most of the youngsters Jerry found appealing.

Jerry made his victims feel special and loved, but he exacted a toll for all that. He "would put his hand on my leg, basically like I was his girlfriend," Victim Number 4 told the jury. "It freaked me out extremely bad." Victim Number 3 also testified that "the hand on the knee thing happened like right away," in their relationship. "That was a big thing for Jerry."

The pattern itself is so classic that experts in child sexual victimization recognize it readily as "grooming." I will explain more about the phenomenon of grooming in a later chapter. However, the fact that Jerry used textbook methods employed by child sex offenders in and of itself lends credibility to the victims' testimony, as does other evidence and corroborating testimony from people besides the victims.

The emotionality of many of the victims was completely moving and convincing to the jury as well. As one CNN reporter described some of the testimony:

"The words came haltingly, punctuated by ragged sighs, groans and cracking voices as two teenage boys just days out of high school bared their darkest secrets to a packed courtroom.

"One sat up straight, bit his lower lip and then seemed to break down, his slender frame wracked by sobs as he buried his head in his hands. Two days later, the other cracked his knuckles and fidgeted. His childish 'yeahs' and the eye patch he wore over an injury made him seem younger than his years, more vulnerable.

"Neither wanted to be there. Both hung their heads and cried as they described in detail what they said a mentor did to them when they were little boys who needed a father figure. 'He...' the 18-year-old known as Victim No. 1, started to say. The witness hesitated, choking back sobs. 'He put...' Pausing now, he reached for the strength to spit out the words. 'He put his mouth on my privates.'

'Um, he, ah,' began the other 18-year-old, known as Victim No. 9. After a nervous laugh, he described the act of oral sex in graphic terms. Chewing on a thumbnail, he explained, 'That's how you have to put it.' And then he revealed that he was sodomized.

'He got real aggressive, and just forced me into it,' he said. 'And I just went with it; there was no fighting against it.' Sometimes, the witness added, he'd 'scream, tell him to get off me. But you're in a basement, no one can hear you down there.'"[2]

Besides the undeniable reluctance, pain, and authenticity with which the victims told their stories (and I will go into why victims are reluctant to come forward in a later chapter) there were just too many instances of people catching a glimpse of something odd going on with Jerry Sandusky and children for the allegations against him to be false. These incidents particularly surrounded the showers at Penn State's athletic facilities. As far back as 1987, Matt Paknis of the Penn State football coaching staff said that Jerry was "creepy" the way he acted around the kids from The Second Mile that he constantly surrounded himself with.

"I always thought there was something weird about him. It was a boundary issue," Paknis said. He was always touching the kid. You cross the line when you touch kids. You don't put your hands on kids."[3] Himself a survivor of child sexual victimization,

---

[2] Ann O' Neill, CNN, The 'Sandusky 8' describe seduction, molestation, and betrayal. June 17, 2012. Available online at http://www.cnn.com/2012/06/17/justice/sandusky-trial-first-week-wrap/index.html
[3] Bill Moushey and Bob Dvorchak, Game Over (New York: William Morrow, an Imprint of HarperCollinsPublishers, 2012) p. 29.

Paknis wonders if his heightened sensibilities about the issue allowed him to detect something "off" about Jerry before others did.

There were rumors, incidents, and warnings to Jerry not to repeat his shower "horseplay" dating back to 1998 at Penn State, and then there were full-blown accusations by responsible, credible, adult people who had seen actual sexual victimization going on. There was Mike McQueary, who was so shaken by what he saw and heard in the Penn State showers in 2001 that he could barely articulate it to his boss, Joe Paterno. There were the victims—who are some of the bravest men I have ever seen—who were willing to come forth to seek justice and publicly tar the great football icon with the brush he had fashioned for himself. The first of these was Aaron Fisher in 2008, who has written his own book Silent No More. Aaron, his mother, his school, and his psychologist brought what Jerry Sandusky had done to him to the attention of his school principal, Children and Youth Services and, finally, to the police.

In the following chapters, I go into more detail as to why victims of child sexual victimization, particularly males, almost never disclose their victimization to anyone. It is a widespread pattern and the reasons for it are real and compelling. The shame and secrecy of what is done to them behind closed doors silences most children, and this shame follows them into manhood. What is more, as children, they feel totally powerless against their offenders.

It is not surprising at all that when they were children, the victims did not cry out for help or report what Jerry was doing to anyone. Some people act as if that made the victims somehow less credible or even at fault. Victim Number 9 explained in court that he was afraid to cry out for help; that Jerry was so much bigger than he was, he was intimidated. Jerry was "bigger" in stature and we, his victims, all had some vague idea of his power too.

The Paterno-Sandusky juggernaut that was Penn State football during that era brought in millions in clear profit to the university on an annual basis. Beaver Stadium, built during their tenure as coaches, seated over 100,000 people. It is one of the largest stadiums in the country. Jerry had access to it and some proprietary interest in it. It was part of his legacy, and he had the air of a part owner of this imposing edifice, so big it even blocks out the sight of the mountain from some vantage points. Children may not know the details of such eminence, but they can sense it. I can testify to the fact that, if you were at Jerry's side, you could see how much prestige he had, even if you were only eight or nine years old.

Would any child believe he could blow the whistle on this man who could do no wrong in the eyes of Happy Valley, who was a demi-god around campus? Who would believe us—frightened, victimized, already vulnerable and "at risk" children to whom normal society was a very faraway place we only had access to through the very man who was abusing us? If a grown man had a problem articulating what Jerry did in the showers of Penn State, how could an eight, nine, or ten year old boy be expected to do so?

Yet, in the end, it was the voices of victimized children crying out from the grown bodies of wounded young men who were willing to testify against Jerry in a court of justice, who won out. Because of their voices, the biggest scandal in the history of college sports was decided, at long last, in favor of the victims. Truth was spoken to power and truth won.

This is a conversation I had with my "inner child"—the one who too was silent about his victimization for so long, until I grew into a man who could give him a voice and thus empower him with the truth and allow him to grow as a child should grow, unmolested.

* * *

A CONVERSATION WITH MY INNER CHILD:

"Please sit down. I would like to have a talk." I knew I was at a point where I needed to sit down with this young, scared, and lost boy. He needed to hear what I had to say, and I needed to put into words what I had been feeling. We sat there for a quiet moment. I just looked into his empty blue eyes as he returned the stare right back into mine. He was dressed in torn up jeans and a filthy t-shirt that he had worn for the past week. His blonde hair was long and unkempt, like he had just woken up from another restless night where sleep escaped him.

"The first thing I want to say is, I believe you." He was no longer looking at me. "You are the bravest person I have ever met, and I will do all that I can to make sure you no longer get hurt." I know he hears me but there is no reaction.

Is this child that stubborn? Was he never taught to look at someone who is speaking to him? Is he a bad kid with no respect for others? No. I know these things are not true about him. He is scared. He has been afraid for most of his life. It has been a life that taught him to trust no one, especially men. It is a fear that most likely started from birth, but as he has explained to me, his first memory is being around two years old. His alcoholic biological father has him sitting on a bed and is kneeling at his feet, holding the red-hot flame of a cigarette lighter to his tiny, fragile toes. His father, his protector, is causing him excruciating pain. As he cries out, his mother and grandfather are beating on the door. He can hear the panic in their voices as they plead with his father to let him go. As the tears roll down over his little cheeks, he sees that his father is laughing. Then darkness overtakes him completely. This was his beginning.

"Look at me, please. You need to know that I love you and I will never hurt you."

As he looks up at me, I see those blue eyes and I see the tears. In that moment I can't control myself, and we both cry together. I want to hug him but I do not want to invade his boundaries. I am here with him, having the hardest conversation either of us has ever had. It will have to be enough for now. This little boy has experienced so much in his life, and here he is, still standing. I know he won't speak during this conversation. Words have been beaten out of him, and the threats from the offenders are real. It is now my duty to protect this child and give him the opportunity to see a world he has only imagined existed.

After his victimization from his biological father, a man who was supposed to protect him and nurture him, his adoptive father then sexually victimized this innocent boy. I wasn't there to protect him at the time. That would never happen again.

"I want to thank you for what you have done for us. I know you lost your childhood, but now I am giving that back. It is my turn to carry the pain and put it away for good. You are my hero, and I will forever be thankful and inspired by your strength. Always know that none of this was your fault. Now you go play. I have work to do."

As we stood, he hugged me tightly and for the first time I heard his fragile, scared little voice: "I love you." The tears started to roll from my eyes once again.

CHAPTER THREE:

Jerry's Hunting Grounds— The Second Mile

There are dozens of pictures of Jerry Sandusky on the Internet with kids, and most of those kids are from The Second Mile, the charitable program he founded. This was a program designed to identify and recommend underprivileged kids to a summer camp program and Jerry Sandusky's care. These were at-risk kids from troubled homes who needed a boost in life and a vision of what they could become. They also needed a father figure. Jerry is pictured with many kids during activities of that charitable foundation, smiling, laughing, hanging shoulder to shoulder with them, giving them advice, telling them jokes, clapping them on the back, throwing them in pools, and hugging them. In fact Jerry was pictured on the cover of *Sports Illustrated* with one of his young "friends" from The Second Mile. It turned out the boy pictured was one of his victims, Victim Number 4, who testified against Jerry at his trial.

There are touching quotes from Jerry in newspaper stories about changing lives for the better and how it is all about the kids. He even wrote a book about it, ironically called *Touched*. In some cases, kids from The Second Mile were as or more recalcitrant than Mickey Rooney in *Boys Town*, but, like him, some of them came to see the light and went on to college and successful careers because of Jerry Sandusky's charitable program. Jerry was perceived as a modern day Father Flanagan, and he carried the same aura of charitable goodness and love about him.

In retrospect people reflected that his gung-ho attitude about kids, especially certain boys, was a little odd. Others could not have gotten away with inviting children to sit by his side at athletic banquets, to travel out of state with him and stay with him at hotels, and spend numerous overnights at his family home.

The Second Mile gave Jerry a glow of sainthood that protected him from people's normal suspicions about adults who seem to be overly fond of children and who spend disproportionate amounts of time with them.

In some newspaper accounts, the now adult graduates of The Second Mile program openly thanked him for what he had done for them. Some were written up as "giving back" to Jerry by taking him to a sports outing they had paid for all on their own now that they were successful, contributing members of society thanks to Jerry's interventions.

Jerry allowed us to feel good about ourselves as a society that takes care of its less privileged members and helps get them on the right path. Everyone was blinded by the glory of his good deeds and did not see what he was doing to the souls of the children he hand-picked out of The Second Mile for his own gratification.

THE ROTTEN CORE OF A WELL-RESPECTED PROGRAM

Jerry founded The Second Mile in 1977. The organization has said it has served about 100,000 children. It became one of President George H. W. Bush's Thousand Points of Light in 1990 and received other awards and recognition as well.

The Second Mile benefited from its association with Penn State in many ways, including the use of Penn State's golf courses for the Second Mile's annual golf tournament to raise funds. Penn State and NFL football players showed up for Second Mile events, lending their fame to promote the organization. The foundation was worth more than ten million dollars in assets, and luminaries like Mark Wahlberg and Arnold Palmer graced its board of directors, as did other big names from the worlds of sports and entertainment. The donor list reads like a *Who's Who*, and the program generated around three million dollars in proceeds to help disadvantaged children each year.

Of course, these distinctions have all been taken back now; prominent people have stopped associating themselves with the program, and The Second Mile has transferred its assets and programs over to other charities. It has ceased all operations due to the scandal surrounding Jerry because it bears the indelible taint of having served as Jerry's hunting grounds.

In an article in *The New Yorker*, Malcolm Gladwell characterized The Second Mile as "a sophisticated, multimillion-dollar, fully integrated grooming operation, outsourcing to child-care professionals the task of locating vulnerable children."[4] Gladwell notes that *Sports Illustrated*'s Jack McCallum wrote in 1999 that Jerry's Second Mile work led to "a temptation around Happy Valley to canonize him." Thus, it served as a great cover for Jerry's real intentions, and everyone was fooled. Gladwell also notes that Bill Lyon of the *Philadelphia Inquirer* said of Jerry: "He isn't in this business for recognition. His defense plays out in front of millions. But when he opens the door and invites in another stray, there is no audience. The ennobling measure of the man is that he has chosen the work that is done without public notice."

I believe it was a delicate balance between public recognition that Jerry used to keep up the appearances of helping children and privacy that allowed him to sexually victimize boys. The Second Mile was where he carefully cultivated an image of public service, "groomed" victims and their parents, and selected certain boys upon whom he bestowed special favors, knowing full well that they would not tell anyone about what he did to them when they were out of sight.

Gladwell goes on to note: "We now know what Sandusky was really doing with The Second Mile. He was setting up a pipeline of young troubled boys. Just as important, though, he was establishing his bona fides. Psychologists call this 'grooming'— the process by which child molesters ingratiate themselves into the communities they wish to exploit. Gladwell notes that one

4 Malcolm Gladwell, In Plain Sight, *The New Yorker*, September 14, 2012, available online at http://www.newyorker.com/magazine/2012/09/24/in-plain-view

child sexual victimization expert recounted that some molesters confessed to having spent several years getting a community used to their presence, getting to like and trust them, before they would approach any children sexually.

This kind of scheming manipulation is hard to believe of any person. Yet it is common behavior among child sex offenders. As I warn parents in my talks on child sexual victimization, child sex offenders groom their targeted victims, their caretakers, and their environment, which means they groom their preferred children, their parents, and the community in which they live. In fact, the very first step of the grooming process may be to befriend a parent and gain the parent's trust so that the parent becomes blind to them as a potential perpetrator.

It is perhaps hard to believe that Jerry set up The Second Mile for this purpose alone—to find vulnerable children to molest. The fact is, as a "boy-lover" Jerry actually fell in love with his victims. He actually "loves" boys so he most likely set up The Second Mile for dual purposes: to help underserved needy children and to give him access, authority, and control over boys for sex. All of the victims who testified in court and most of those who have come forward since met him through the program. It was his harvesting ground, and, as far as we know, his only one. It provided many victims, almost all from distressed home situations were an over-burdened single parent found it hard to properly supervise a boy, and where a protective father was nowhere to be seen. The Second Mile children were easy pickings for Jerry Sandusky.

I don't mean to disparage the program or the good it did in turning around some young lives and providing benefits for others. The Second Mile was aimed at helping disadvantaged youth reach their maximum potential so they could be successful in life. The program took "at risk" youth out of their environments and teamed them up with older individuals to help show them all the possibilities that life offered. The program also tried to work with the parents to give their youth a better chance at success in

life. School guidance counselors were usually the people who referred troubled students to The Second Mile, and many of these
children were genuinely helped by it.

In my case, it was hoped that the program would raise my
self-esteem, because one of its stated aims was to build self-con-
fidence in youth. My school guidance counselor also noted I had
trust issues with grown males, and that The Second Mile would
expose me to men I could put my faith in.

I need not even comment on the irony of that. In the end, of
course, The Second Mile program exposed me to the exact opposite of what it intended to. It destroyed what little self-esteem
I had, and trusting adults, particularly grown men, became more
difficult than ever before. That was not because of The Second
Mile per se, though. It was because of Jerry Sandusky.

The Second Mile was eerily like what FBI agent Kenneth
Lanning said such programs run or staffed by child molesters can
be: a venue that gives the molester access to plenty of victims. It
can be a hunting ground for an offender looking for vulnerable
prey. Such a program can also, as Lanning pointed out, serve
to assuage the molesters' guilt: "Their need to rationalize their
sexual interests and behavior often leads them to be involved in
'good works' that help troubled, needy children." Because they
believe they are doing so much for children, the sexual favors
they take are justified in their own minds. They may perceive
the sexual liberties they take with children as their just reward.
Or they may feel that the love and time they pour out on these
children is the main part of what they do in these programs, and
the sexual victimization is just a small, unimportant part of all
they share.

As I've mentioned, The Second Mile added to Jerry's already
towering stature in the community and thus protected him from
detection. What a great guy, everyone thought. What a truly self-
less person to want to give to underprivileged, "at risk" kids the
things they'd never had—a solid father figure, a mentor, a wealthy
and powerful person who cared about them and could give them

experiences they would otherwise never have, like tickets to Penn State games, meeting the players, travel to college bowls, and the use of Penn State's top-of-the-line athletic facilities.

In fact, as I mentioned, Jerry Sandusky had won presidential recognition for his exemplary Second Mile program and numerous other awards in regard to it. Here Jerry was, a wealthy and powerful man, yet he spent his spare time mentoring underprivileged kids in order to give back to the community. Jerry seemed to be the epitome of what American success looked like—athletic, competitive, winning, and yet philanthropic.

While the program did a lot of good for many children, it was also, unfortunately, Jerry's hunting grounds for finding children that fit his specific sexual interests and it served as a way of gaining access to them. This fits the profile of child sexual offenders in a textbook way.

Jim Clemente, who has already been mentioned, was a prosecutor for the New York City Law Department and an FBI profiler who has worked numerous sex crimes cases and is a recognized expert on child sexual victimization. He noted in his report that Jerry Sandusky "loved kids, and it showed." It did. The pictures of Jerry on the Internet with "friends" show a man full of joy in the company of kids. His great love for children was also part of his reputation as a guy with a heart of gold, one of the few people willing to help underprivileged children by giving of his love, his time, his labor, and his money. The fact that Jerry loved kids was evident. The problem was that his love spilled over into the sexual; he found kids too attractive, too stimulating, and he acted on those impulses.

Jerry was a perfect example of a "pillar of the community boy lover." This is a type of offender who not only actually helps underprivileged boys but actually falls in love with them. He treats them like they are his "boyfriends" and is heartbroken when they pull away from him. This is evident when we look at how he treated those of us most close to him, and how when we tried to distance ourselves he turned to stalking techniques to maintain his power and control over us.

Indeed, if "loving boys" in the wrong way wasn't the entire reason behind the existence of The Second Mile, it was a big part of it. The founding of The Second Mile was definitely due to Jerry's desire for a personal hunting ground full of vulnerable kids that he had unfettered access and control over.

JERRY'S RETIREMENT FROM PENN STATE GAVE HIM MORE TIME FOR THE SECOND MILE

Jerry retired from coaching in 1999 to spend yet more time helping The Second Mile. Indeed, Joe Paterno had told him that he would never suggest that Penn State hire Jerry to replace him as head coach because he couldn't serve two masters—The Second Mile and coaching football, because Jerry was already so deeply involved in his activities with underprivileged children. Sometimes he even brought his little "friends" along to coach's meetings. The Second Mile seemed at least as important to him, perhaps more so, than his chosen career of football coaching.

Some people find the circumstances of Jerry's retirement from football coaching a little odd. The timing coincided with the very first report about an incident with a young male child by the child's mother. The mother notified the university in 1998 that, from what she was hearing, Jerry's contact with her child was highly inappropriate. She was a single mother, and she had thought that Jerry and his Second Mile program would be excellent for her son, who had been a participant for several years when the inappropriate incident occurred. Jerry invited the boy to the gym at PSU to work out. They lifted weights, then Jerry told him he wanted to "work on some wrestling moves." Then he took him to the showers.

After Jerry brought her son home to her, as the boy was walking away from her on his way to his bedroom, he said, "In case you're wondering, my hair is wet because I showered with Jerry Sandusky." The mother knew her son and realized that when he was really upset and uncertain about something, he made similar "throw away" statements because he did not know how do deal with some issues head on. She waited a few minutes, then went to talk to her son.

The boy explained that Jerry had taken him into the showers. She saw no reason why her son should have been taken to a shower, and her child's account of other things that occurred that evening unnerved her so much, she came to think that Jerry Sandusky should be arrested.

Alone in the deserted athletic complex, Jerry had had the woman's son needlessly change into another pair of shorts. I know from my own experience that Jerry preferred "his" boys to wear shorts. This made them easier to access. Jerry also needlessly pressed the boy to shower after a brief wrestling match, and he made sure the boy showered right next to him. During the shower, Jerry had hugged the boy tightly, from the back and the front, while the two were naked. Then he had lathered him up with soap by hand. The boy was uncomfortable throughout the incident, and he also did not like it that, on the drive home, Jerry's hand was on his thigh.

Alarmed, the mother called her friend and psychotherapist, a Dr. Chambers, who interviewed the boy and wrote up a summary report stating in part that Jerry Sandusky's behavior displayed all the "red flag" behaviors of a child sex offender. She went to her boss at The Department of Children and Youth Services (DCYS), who immediately recognized a conflict of interest with this case. DCYS had placed two dozen foster children and half a dozen adoptive children in Jerry's home and many thousands of children into The Second Mile. So, her boss referred the case to the State Department of Public Welfare for investigation.

Unfortunately, the DPW engaged a "psychologist" named Seasock to evaluate the boy and Jerry Sandusky. They did not know, apparently, that although Seasock was holding himself out as a licensed and credentialed psychologist, he had not yet earned his degree in psychology. After interviewing both the boy and

Jerry, Seasock erroneously concluded that Jerry Sandusky could not be a "pedophile" because 1. He had never heard of a man becoming a pedophile at age 57 (completely ignoring the fact that most child sex crimes go unreported for many decades) 2. Although, Jerry did make the boy change clothes, he allowed the boy to change in a different area of the locker room (completely ignoring the fact that Jerry knew that the boy would soon be completely naked in the shower with him, and ignoring the fact that the shorts Jerry gave the boy might have been specifically chosen to increase Jerry's access to the boy's genitals, and 3. Jerry's self-reported lack of sexual intent (most offenders will not admit to sexual intent in such an interview when they know they can be prosecuted for it).

Seasock's report effectively torpedoed any chance of an effective prosecution against Jerry. The State's own "expert" in the field had determined and written a report stating that Jerry had no sexual intent; instead he simply had boundary issues. Simply put, Seasock had determined that Jerry Sandusky didn't realize that it was out of line to horse around while showering with boys at the gym. The DA declined to prosecute and instructed the University Police Department chief to admonish Jerry to cease his practice of showering with boys anywhere.

These professionals apparently believed that this was the proper solution to the issue. The ultimate decision by the District Attorney, the Department of Public Welfare, the Department of Children and Youth Services, and the University Police Department was that there was no criminal violation and no charges were to be filed.

Jerry's use of the showers and athletic facilities at Penn State thus went on unabated for several more years, and he victimized other boys there too. This is a sad reality.

When people don't know what is going on, they can't stop it. But here, certainly, the officials were remiss. They did nothing to make sure his privileges at the Penn State athletic facilities were revoked. They left it up to Jerry to self-police his showering with boys and "horsing around" behavior based on their belief that he was an honest, trustworthy man. They were obviously dead wrong, and the boys who were victimized suffered because of it.

We must demand that every youth serving organization be mandated to train their employees and volunteers about these issues and in that way help to prevent it in the future. It is inexcusable that these responsible departments did not do more to protect children from Jerry Sandusky.

Was Jerry's precipitous retirement—when he was Joe Paterno's heir apparent to the throne of being Penn State's head football coach—just the university's way of trying to get rid of something that was starting to look like a hot potato by passing it on as fast as they could? Was this Penn State's response to rumors of molestation—to move the person around a little, shift the sands a little, and hope for the best? If so, this was much the way the Catholic Church responded to reports of child molestation among its priests, and it is reprehensible.

However, I think Jerry knew exactly what he was doing when he retired. He knew that Paterno would never pick him as his replacement head coach because of his continued major time commitment with The Second Mile. He also knew that no other university would be willing to hire him if he split his time and attention between football and The Second Mile. His options were minimal. He may have gotten a scare with his close call with the 1998 victim and wanted to fade out of the Penn State picture. On top of that, the University's retirement package offered a great deal to any employee with thirty years on the job. Then there was that interesting bonus payment of $176,000.00, which he gave to The Second Mile so they could purchase some land from PSU.

A change in employment status, though, does not unmake a child sex offender. They will go on to molest again. Whatever the real circumstances of his retirement, Jerry left his position with Penn State to spend more time with children in The Second Mile, which seemed to be his most important priority.

Jerry's retirement from coaching did not include being barred from the Penn State facilities. Far from it. He had a life-long pass to the athletic department, its equipment, and showers. He had an on-campus office. He had access to games. These were the kinds of benefits he continued to use to groom "his" kids from The Second Mile.

"Nice Guy Offenders"

I've noted that one of the reasons Jerry could go on so long as a child sex offender was the fact that he was perceived as a highly charitable guy because of The Second Mile. This is not rare for a child sex offender.

Clemente noted that Jerry fell into the category of "nice guy" acquaintance sex offenders, an all-too-common category that can include clergy, coaches, teachers, babysitters, favorite uncles, friends of the family, and others we would never suspect. The pervert of "stranger danger" fame, wearing the raincoat and hanging around the playground is largely a myth. Most child sex offenders do love children (in their own perverted and criminal way). They love to be around them, and it shows. They often involve themselves in activities with youth so as to have access to those they find so appealing.

The "nice guy offender syndrome" contributes to the idea of the "compliant victim," as Clemente characterizes children who are groomed into silence and don't immediately run to authorities after an incident of sexual victimization (in fact, most victims of child sex crimes do not report the victimization to parents or authorities). Like most child sex offenders, Jerry didn't have horns and a tail. He understood kids and, as mentioned, he genuinely enjoyed being around them. A great deal of his time was spent mentoring them and providing fun and character-building activities for them, especially kids who didn't have dads around. Hanging around with him could be great, and he was generous with his gifts of cool, athletically themed clothing, shoes, tickets and rides to events, food, and privileges. He wasn't all bad. Many kids liked him a great deal. He was definitely a nice guy.

Yet over time it became clear that behind Jerry's benevolent smile and kind deeds was lust for young boys. Only time revealed that The Second Mile, while it definitely did some good, was also a hunting ground for him to find his victims. Only time revealed that his unlimited access to the fine athletic facilities of Penn State, including the locker rooms and showers, gave him multiple opportunities to sexually assault boys while supposedly sharing the wonders of the university's athletic department with them. It is sad that time also revealed that much of his generosity to his victims was a phenomenon called "grooming," when a child sexual offender gains the trust of his victims (and their parents and their community) by his acts of kindness, so that they become indebted to him and used to ever-escalating levels of physical intimacy.

JERRY CHOOSES ME

I'm one of the kids in those Second Mile pictures with Jerry. I was a Second Miler. There are some pictures with me where Jerry is just beaming with joy as he holds my hand.

Maybe it was my flaxen hair. Maybe it was my radiant face and smile and how alive and happy I seemed. I was overjoyed at The Second Mile. I was totally thrilled to be with so many other kids at the summer camps The Second Mile sponsored. The rooms were clean, the food was plentiful, and the activities were great. There was plenty of good sports equipment not to mention the fabulous facilities of Penn State. My family could never have afforded such a great camp for me. I was in paradise there.

Jerry picked me out of hundreds of kids to bestow his favors and attention upon. It was super flattering at the time, of course. I later learned that I fit the profile of the type of kid Jerry preferred sexually. Nearly all of his victims were, of course, very young, aging from eight or nine years old to fifteen years. (Fifteen years was about the age most of us could no longer put up with his actions as our own sexual identities emerged and we came to know full well that what Jerry was doing was wrong.) To be one of "his" boys, we had to be young and unknowing, innocent and confused by his sexual advances rather than being certain they were off the wall. He preferred tow-headed boys with angelic faces and delicate features. He liked kids who were skinny and a little fragile-looking. Since most of his victims from The Second Mile were from broken homes, that air of fragility could come from being young, undeveloped, and slender (maybe even underfed) but it was also communicated emotionally. We were psychologically fragile too; we were less sturdy inside than kids from more stable backgrounds. We were probably more prone to doubt ourselves and our perception of things. I'm sure that Jerry's preferred victim type included those boys who were anxious to gain and keep adult attention and nurturing.

Because Jerry liked his victims vulnerable, boys from broken homes were easy pickings. We were hungry for a father figure, economically deprived, and most of us belonged to households where an overworked and over-stressed single mother was in charge and all too happy to find someone willing to mentor her boy while she worked or took care of her other kids. Most single mothers are looking for good adult male role models for their sons. What better role model than football king and community benefactor Jerry Sandusky? What better program than Jerry's The Second Mile, designed especially for kids from distressed homes? We were ripe for Jerry's picking.

As a favored member of The Second Mile, I became like a part of Jerry's family, with plenty of time spent at his home, in his car, on the road with him, and on overnights. He formally adopted me at age eighteen because the name Sandusky would give me a golden ticket in life, as we both figured, including reduced tuition at Penn State. By age eighteen I could legally overcome my mother's long term and strenuous objections to anyone adopting me.

I was Jerry's foster son in more than a legal way, though. Throughout my adolescence, I had lived in his home for several years, under his court-ordered supervision. I knew him well. I was a part of his family. I was in Jerry's snare physically, emotionally, and mentally. I was the perfect prey.

CHAPTER FOUR:

The Perfect Prey

What kind of children become the prey of child sex offenders? Children like I was are often the perfect prey. Yet if we are going to talk about prey, we must talk about predators. Yet in fact, "predator" is something of a misnomer, and it is misleading.

The term sexual "predator" is a great fit when we are talking about "stranger danger" and child abductors who prey on kids. However, with "Nice guy" acquaintance offenders, that term is misleading. It allows the Jerry Sanduskys of this world to get away with their sex crimes against kids because people simply don't see them as predators. "Predator" is an emotionally loaded term that acts as a shield for offenders who smile in the faces of their victims and guardians and win their trust over a period of time, and who are genuinely nice guys except for the abuse. This is your typical child sex offender; far more typical than the stranger in the raincoat, the abductor near the merry-go-round, the predator who drags the kids into the forest.

Child sexual victimization is more common than we think, so there is no prototypical victim; it happens to children of all ages, races, ethnicities, cultures, and economic backgrounds. Child sexual victimization occurs in rural, urban, and suburban areas. It affects both girls and boys in all kinds of neighborhoods and communities, and in countries around the world. Girls are at a slightly higher risk than boys (although statistics regarding this may be skewed because so many boys fail to report sexual victimization). Boys are, however, more likely to be sexually victimized by someone outside of, yet known to, their family. Child sexual victimization happens everywhere, all the time.

It is also important to note that while women do sexually victimization children (some 14% of cases reported by boys involve female perpetrators as are some 6% of such cases reported by girls. Yet the strong majority of cases involve male offenders. Male offenders may prey upon boys or girls. Therefore, for the most part, when I talk about a child sexual offender in this book, I will use forms of the pronoun "he."

In spite of prevalent warnings about "stranger danger," in fact, most children are sexually victimized by someone they know and trust. The majority of perpetrators of child sexual crimes are familiar to the child but are not members of the child's family. They are people who have direct contact with the children, though, often on a regular basis. This would include friends of the family, babysitters, childcare providers, or neighbors. Another significant portion of perpetrators are relatives. The offender may be a child's own father or mother, or the victimization may come from extended family members such as siblings, cousins, uncles, or aunts. A small minority of perpetrators are strangers to the child, rendering the old admonition to children not to take candy from a stranger incomplete. Warning children about only a small percentage of the real dangers that are out there, leaves them more vulnerable to victimization from the "good" people that they know and trust. Importantly, most stranger sexual assaults are single events, whereas most acquaintance offenders groom their victims into a long-term course of victimization that includes multiple offenses over the course of days, weeks, months or years.We need to empower kids with that information so that they know where the danger really comes from and so they know they have the right and power to tell someone if something is about to or has happened.   Here are some of the numbers: there are only about 160 long term stranger child abductions in the U.S. each year. There are about 2,000 short term, less that 15 minutes, non-familial abductions a year. There are estimates of 200,000 to 300,000 child molestations a year. That means that Stranger Danger is only about 1% of the cases each year.

What's more, perpetrators do contact children through their computers, so giving children cyber smarts is as important as telling a child not to talk to strangers. In fact, telling kids not to "talk to strangers" in the electronic age is particularly ineffective, because most kids don't think that a person that they are chatting with online for days, weeks, months or years is a "stranger" any more.

Not all perpetrators are full grown adults. Teenagers and sometimes younger children sexually victimize other children. However, most teen sex crimes cases are sealed and not subject to data collection, so exact numbers and percentages are hard to come by. That does not mean parents should not be vigilant about the other children and teenagers they let their children hang around with, though; in fact, it means the opposite.

What kind of children, if any, are likely to be sexually victimized? There are some patterns to be noted. The National Association of School Psychologists says that the child who is most likely to be sexually victimized is someone who has been victimized before or who is otherwise psychologically vulnerable and needy because of a chaotic family of origin. This condition results in low self-esteem and is often accompanied by a lack of parental involvement and supervision in their lives, making such children more vulnerable to offenders.

That said, some offenders target kids who are outstanding students or athletes with outgoing personalities because they may be more adventurous and bold in regard to experimenting with new behaviors or they may be more rebellious in terms of acting outside the prescribed norms.

In some ways, according to the NASP standards, I was the perfect prey. I was the good-looking yet psychologically vulnerable kid—the needy kid hungering for a father figure, the kid who would look up at a powerful man like Jerry Sandusky with yearning, with wide open eyes that had already seen many scenes of childhood victimization and were looking for some sort of peace, safety, adult guidance, and support.

Victimization at the Hands of My Father

My biological father physically victimized me for many years. He was an alcoholic who had a fearsome temper. He would often come home drunk and beat my mother. When he would get tired of hitting her, I became the target of his victimization. He hated me, and I can't even really tell you the reason why. Surely, as such a young child, I could not have invited so much anger to rain down on my head. His problems came from within him, but somehow, as the oldest of his children, I was next in line after my mother to suffer his victimization.

Maybe having kids was too much responsibility for an alcoholic, who is having trouble taking responsibility even for himself. Maybe he felt guilty, as I am told most alcoholics do. Clearly, he knew somewhere in his heart that he owed it to his children to be a better father. Sometimes when the presence of another person makes someone feel guilty, the person's behavior toward that person becomes worse and worse. The more guilty he felt, the more I was a living reminder of how he had neglected and victimized our family. Alcoholics also go through personality changes—they know they are failing in life and bringing all kinds of problems down on their own heads, yet they can't seem to stop drinking. So they lash out in anger and frustration, looking for someone—anyone—to blame for the terrible situations they create for themselves.

Whatever the reasons for my father's continual victimization, I have only a few memories of him. None one of them are good.

When I was one year old, my brother was born, and then by the time I was two I had a little sister as well. As I remember it, my brother and sister were never beaten. I was the one who was singled out—the oldest, the first, the biggest, even though I was only a two-year-old boy when he started violently abusing me. The victimization lasted until I was six years old. At that time my dysfunctional parents decided to go their separate ways and get a divorce. I only remember seeing my father two more times after that in my life. I can't even say whether he is still alive or not, and frankly, it does not matter to me. We have and had nothing resembling what should be the relationship between a father and son.

After the divorce my mother, my siblings, and I had to move in with my grandparents on my mother's side. My grandparents' home was a four-bedroom, 1800 square foot home with no running water or working plumbing. A large, gray, plastic 55-gallon canister collected rainfall from a downspout on the back porch, and that was our water source. Our bathroom consisted of a 5-gallon bucket.

There were seven adults and ten children living in the home. The entire house was infested with little brown cockroaches. We avoided the basement due to the rats living there that were literally the size of small dogs.

Taught Silence at the Handle of a Broom

My grandfather was a war veteran who had a mean streak. I don't remember him ever being nice to anyone, or smiling, so maybe it wasn't just a streak. Maybe it was the way he was, through and through. He was a very abusive man, and he was the disciplinarian in the home. Any time we did something that we needed to be reprimanded for, he would call us into his bedroom. He had an old, wooden broom handle that he would smack us with. He would swing it wildly and whoever or wherever it hit didn't matter. You also were expected not to cry, or the beating would continue until you stopped. Whether you were guilty or not, you were to accept the punishment in as much silence as you could muster. Talking back was something you just didn't do.

Maybe this also contributed to my inability to disclose, my inability to speak up to Jerry or to another adult about Jerry's victimization. I had been taught, at the end of a broom handle, that you kept your mouth shut when an adult was misusing you.

We teach our kids to listen to adults, especially adults in positions of authority. We also need to teach kids that people in positions of authority and trust may abuse that authority and trust and if they do, they can and will be held accountable. This will help potential victims know there is the possibility of threat even from trusted people, so that they can more easily recognize sexual abuse when it is coming, and hopefully avoid being victimized. At the very least, teaching them well can make them feel confident that if child sexual victimization does happen, they have the right to stand up and report it so it can be stopped and the offender can be brought to justice.

My grandmother was the exact opposite of my grandfather. She was a beautiful, kind woman who did her best to clean, cook, and keep the family running as smoothly as possible. She was an amazing cook. I loved it when she made homemade bread. Walking into the filthy home could be pleasant when you were totally enveloped with the sweet smell of butter and fresh fried bread dough. Those smells are some of my fondest memories. Also, she would have us kids go out into the woods behind the home and pick wild raspberries. She would then bake homemade raspberry pies from scratch and serve them to us fresh out of the oven, with a big scoop of vanilla ice cream.

Because of my grandmother, in the midst of hell, we had our small bites of heaven too. Maybe this is what gave me a glimpse of how life could and should be. Maybe this helped me see that I too deserved a good life and to be loved.

In this home I witnessed a lot of family violence. If you were upset with someone you used your fists; words, reasoning, and common sense never counted for much; in fact, they barely existed in that house.

There was sexual victimization too. One of my aunts would pimp her son out to a man on the weekends for money. I also saw an uncle sexually abusing my female cousins, although at the age I witnessed this, I was not old enough to understand what it was or even how wrong and illegal it was. I can only pray that my cousins have received the help they deserve. They went through the same hell I was to go through.

My mother tried her best to keep my brother, sister, and me safe, but she just couldn't do it. We would be left with people who were not qualified to be watching children. At other times we were left all alone, even at very young ages.

At times my mother would find some kind of work, and each time she did we were able to move out of my grandparents' home and into our own place. That was always promising and exciting, but it always ended the same way. At some point she would quit her job, and eventually we would get evicted from our home for non-payment of rent, and then we would be back in with my grandparents.

I watched my mother steal many times. The exact purpose as to why she did this is not something I can know for sure. Most times that I witnessed it happening, it seemed it was objects that she desired more than objects that we needed for survival. I learned from an early age that if you couldn't afford something, you stole it, because that was what my mother did. Stealing became a way of life for me.

I remember one time my grandparents picked us up from school and told us our mother had been arrested for stealing and would be in jail for the next thirty days. I don't believe I have ever cried so hard in my life. It was the first time in my life that I felt totally alone.

Yet nobody told us that stealing was wrong and that there could be terrible consequences. It became a daily behavior for me.

The first time I remember stealing something was a pack of gum from a convenience store. I was so scared, my hands were shaking uncontrollably. From there I would steal food from a supermarket or steal desirable, luxury items from friends. I graduated from petty theft to breaking into buildings to steal larger items. I was never very good at stealing and I was arrested quite often for my crimes. This type of behavior, along with my chaotic home life, ensured that I became well known to the police and to child protective services.

It was always amazing to me, though, that no matter what conditions I was living in or what behavior I displayed, I was never taken away and placed in a safe home. We would visit child protective services regularly. They would interview my brother, sister, and myself separately. We were never going to tell what was happening to us. Yet they expected that we would. We were afraid that if they found out, they would split us up, and that we would never see each other again. Our lips were sealed.

I do not pretend to know how the Child Protective Services operates or what guidelines they must follow. I can only speak to you from my point of view as a child caught up in the system. When I was taken into a room by myself with a strange adult and asked to "rat" my mom out, that simply was not an option. Even though, my mother didn't supply us with much, I still loved her and would not hurt her. In my early life I saw law enforcement and CPS as the enemy. I saw their arrogance when they spoke to us and how they spoke down to my mother. They made it easy to hate them.

Children are very good at reading non-verbal cues, and coming where I came from, I became an expert of sorts. My mother, brother, and sister were all that I knew, and I was not going to risk splitting us up no matter how bad our circumstances were. What was more, physical punishment at home might follow any "reporting" I did to CPS. Those people expected us to spill our guts then go home with the person whom we just had exposed. They offered us no real protection.

I am thankful there are people doing the work to protect children. There are never enough, and they are overworked and underpaid. I get that, and I do not mean to be critical, but such people must realize that they have an opportunity to shape a child's life with how they do their jobs. I think that we could all learn to live with a little more compassion and empathy towards one another, but especially towards children.

Because I never experienced that type of approach—one of compassion and understanding for both me and for my family—I figured it was up to them to investigate. I wouldn't help. I was never removed, and it seems that no help was ever offered to myself or any member of my family. The guidelines must have been pretty lax to allow us to remain placed in the environment we were growing up in. It's hard to imagine that any foster home placement would have been worse.

Yet, while much of my childhood was not what any child should experience, I did have times when I loved life. My brother, Ron, and I would always be together. We were brothers but we were also best friends. We would play catch out in the front yard. I would be Jay Bell of the Pittsburgh Pirates, and he would be Lenny Dykstra of the Philadelphia Phillies, our favorite team and players at the time. We would go to the old junkyard and get two old inner tubes from tractor-trailer tires and spend the day floating down the creek. One time I remember I had broken my foot playing football, but we still decided to float down the creek. We came upon a spot where there is a waterfall of sorts, and one of us was going to have to jump out and pull the other to the side of the creek. I had a cast on my foot and wasn't supposed to get it wet so I nominated my brother, but for some reason he was not interested in jumping into the deep muddy water to pull us to safety. As we neared the waterfall I had no choice but to jump into the creek and pull us to safety, soaking my cast.   I remember hunting and fishing with Ron. I was never very good at sitting still and waiting for a fish to nibble at the bait or for a deer to come into my line of sight, but my brother loved it, and so I would go so that we could be together. We had a bond that couldn't be broken, or so I thought. If someone started a fight with me they started it with him and vice versa.

We once had an older cousin who was driving us home in a snowstorm and he clipped another car. He panicked and told my brother and I we needed to get out of there before the police showed up because we would be taken away. So we ran into the snow, which was almost up to our knees. At one point we were standing in the middle of what seemed to be a road, frozen to our cores. We eventually realized we were on a major interstate as we saw a tractor-trailer coming at us. Eventually, we would make it home and thaw out and laugh about our cousin's illogical reaction as we explained to our mother what had happened. This is how it was, though, with my brother. It didn't matter what we were doing as long as we were doing it together. We made the life we were living more bearable just being together. That relationship would last for most of my childhood, but it would be ripped apart by Jerry Sandusky.

GOING TO "HAWAII"

School was one of my escapes from my daily life. I excelled in school and I loved going. I was able to get food, play and be with friends, and, best of all, I discovered books. Books were my saving grace at that young age. Through books I could go anywhere and be anyone that I wanted to be. For a young boy coming from the environment I was in, it was amazing to be able to escape into the world of books. I would read about places like Hawaii and dream of what it would be like to sit on the beach with the sun beating down on me. In my child's mind, I knew that Hawaii was not a place that I would ever get to, but it was a place I could escape to in my head when I needed to flee reality. I had mental pictures of Hawaii from the books I had seen, and I became very good at detaching from my physical self during a beating by my grandfather. Mentally, I would go to Hawaii. Little did I know how often I would use this skill to escape other, far more invasive, forms of victimization in the future.

School also allowed for one other thing in my life: guidance counselors. There was one who had seen enough of my behaviors by the time I was seven years old to recommend me to a program she thought would help me. As it stated in the referral, I needed to work on my self-esteem and trust of older males. It was true that from my experience with my father and grandfather I found it very hard to trust grown males. As to self-esteem, I had almost none. I was so cowed by life that even my younger brother would beat me up all the time as a younger child, and I would not defend myself. I barely felt like a whole person.

The program the guidance counselor recommended me to was called "The Second Mile" and it was founded and run by the well-known and highly respected Penn State assistant football coach, Jerry Sandusky, who just loved to help troubled, needy children...

SECOND MILE PARADISE

This troubled, needy child attended weekly programs that The Second Mile hosted. Sometimes it was a picnic at a park; sometimes it was bowling or a holiday party at a high school or a fraternity house on campus. Those were good times. I just loved The Second Mile. I got to go places and do things I would never have been able to do otherwise. I thought it was a wonderful program.

During the summers The Second Mile offered a week-long camp. I would go stay at the Penn State University campus and live in the dorms for a week with a couple of hundred other poor, disadvantaged youth. It was absolutely wonderful.

The first year of camp was such a blessing. Being away from my routine life, I felt very special. There were showers with hot running water and clean rooms. I was given my very own bed, I had three meals a day, and there were plenty of other kids to make friends with. It was a dream come true. It was like being let out of purgatory and entering paradise.

In the evenings the entire camp would visit the Penn State football office and meet in a large group. It was here that I was first introduced to Jerry Sandusky. He would stand up in the front and tell jokes and riddles. He was funny and seemed like a great guy. Everyone loved him. I never spoke to him that first year. I just sat back and watched as he had fun with all the kids. Along with the nightly jokes, I would see him at the pool, tossing kids around, and everyone was laughing. I didn't have the courage or the sense of self to participate that first year.

I was crushed when that first week of summer camp ended. It was time to return to my sad and difficult reality after having a week of glimpsing a different and better life. It was like going from light into darkness. There was the next year's summer camp to look forward to, but that seemed such a long time away.

Still, time went on, and soon it was time for another week of The Second Mile summer camp. I was so excited!

SECOND YEAR AT THE SECOND MILE—JERRY FINDS ME ATTRACTIVE

This year, summer camp was very different. Suddenly I became the object of a lot of Jerry's attention. He seemed to pick me out of hundreds of other boys. While the year before he hadn't even spoken to me, this year he introduced himself to me personally one night before the camp meeting. Also, he started trying to get me involved in activities in the pool.

At the time I didn't notice that every time he picked me up to throw me, his hand would be on my butt or between my legs. It wasn't something I gave much thought to at the time. It was what I had seen him doing the year before with other kids. I didn't have any sense at nine years old that what he was doing was wrong–that he was actually molesting me. By doing it in such a public way, he was cleverly desensitizing me to him touching my genitals. After all, I had seen him doing the exact same thing to other boys last year and no one else complained. So, I figured it must be okay.

I have come to realize now as an adult that those times in the pool were when the sexual victimization began. This is when Jerry also began to "groom" me as his prey for more severe victimization.

CHAPTER FIVE:

Jerry Grooms Me for Victimization

G rooming is a well-known phenomenon to those who study child sexual victimization. It is the way perpetrators operate. It is the textbook modus operandi of child sexual offenders.

Let me take a moment to explain "grooming." Some experts say that the word "seduction" would do just as well to describe what a child sexual offender does to his victim (as mentioned before, a child sexual offender is more frequently a man; thus I use the pronoun "his"). I find the term "seduction" is much more appropriate when the offender and victim are of opposite genders or the victim is questioning his or her sexual identity or identifies as homosexual and the victim and offender are the same gender. This is so because the child may become convinced that the offender has "fallen in love" with the victim and wants to be with the victim for the rest of their lives. However, since the victim will soon "age out" of the offender's desired age range, this will eventually break the child's heart, as the offender always intended to use the child for his or her sexual desires and then move on to another vulnerable child.

Therefore, I am not sure about the term seduction in cases like mine, but grooming I understand perfectly. It is, quite simply, when the would-be molester starts to get the chosen victim to trust him and to get used to being touched by him. The small physical liberties are just little preludes to what is to come. They lull the victim into a sense that being touched by this person is okay. Many times these initial "innocent" touches are done in public and right in front of other children or adults, lending the imprimatur of legitimacy to them. Or, the touching starts out in a completely harmless way, as do the more frequent contacts with the person, and the gifts and privileges associated with being with him.

Grooming reminds me of the story about the frog in hot water. If you put a frog in boiling hot water to stew him, he'll do everything he can to get out. Yet if you put a frog in cool water and just raise the temperature a little bit at a time, by the time the water is boiling, the frog will be trapped and unable to jump out. The frog didn't notice the gradual heating up of the water until it was too late.

Grooming a victim for child sexual victimization is like gradually heating the water the frog is in. The temperature is being turned up just a little at a time. The unsuspecting child may sense something is a little bit off, but the water is not hot enough to cause enough alarm to jump or run away. Young children are innocent of sexuality, anyway. Often they are not sure what the offender is doing and why he is doing it. Their sense of it being wrong or weird may grow stronger, but they still can't quite sort out why. Meanwhile, the water gets hotter and hotter, and by the time children realize that they have been sexually victimized, they feel shame and embarrassment that they let it get this far. Most often, they then choose to remain silent as a way of protecting themselves from the ramifications of public disclosure of that shameful activity.

Jerry groomed children in a textbook way. He grew close to them, gaining their trust and even gaining their parents' trust, by being nice, helpful, and giving. The touching started in seemingly innocent ways: a little horsing around (as Jerry was to call it), a little wrestling, an arm slung over the shoulders, hugs, a hair wash or soap fight in the showers, swatting the rear end, giving the stomach raspberries that make children laugh so hard, and tickling (Jerry always claimed he was The Tickle Monster). At first it would be a hand on the knee while seated next to him the car, and then it would a hand on the thigh . . . Child sex offenders are masters at grooming children for sexual purposes, leading them like the Pied Piper down the slippery slope that starts out with seemingly normal human affection and nurturing.

By the end of the week-long camp during my second summer at The Second Mile, Jerry was taking me upstairs to his office in the building, away from all the other campers and counselors. This made me feel very special – to be singled out for this kind of personal attention from the man in charge was overwhelming. In most camps nowadays, that alone would be considered suspicious behavior, and there should be rules preventing adults from taking a child away from the others and isolating him or her in a deserted part of a building. At least I would hope so. But even if there were such rules at The Second Mile it wouldn't have mattered. Jerry was king there. He made his own rules.

During those conversations he would talk to me about my home life. He would ask how school was going and also things about the camp. He would show great personal interest in me, and it was flattering. I hadn't received much adult attention that was that positive. I was not used to someone so powerful and wealthy being interested in me as an individual.

I also started seeing Jerry around the dorms in the evenings when we were getting ready for lights out. He would come by and say goodnight to the campers.

At one point Jerry asked me if I might be interested in attending a Penn State football game in the fall. What would any male child of that age say? Of course, I said yes. I couldn't believe my luck! I remember being totally excited to tell my friends and family that I would be getting to go to a real college football game. That simple opportunity was something beyond my wildest dreams.

I was feeling so special because of Jerry's attentions. I thought maybe my luck in life was changing. He seemed like the greatest thing that had ever happened to me...

First Football Game at Penn State

It was a beautiful, sunny day in early fall. It was a Saturday, and I couldn't contain my excitement. I felt like a kid on Christmas Eve. I was going to attend my first Penn State football game!

When Jerry showed up to pick me up, you'd better believe I jumped in the car, raring to go. Yet the very first thing I noticed after the hellos was that Jerry placed his right hand on my leg right above my knee. He grabbed it tightly and acted as though he was playing a game, just horsing around. But his hand stayed there. We were on our way to pick up other kids, and I had a very strong feeling of weirdness due to his hand resting on my leg.

I told myself that this must just be something his family did; it was normal to them. I knew that the life and family I had known would never be considered normal, so I conceded that I probably had no idea of how average families acted. We never showed love to one another in my family. There were no kisses goodnight, no hugs goodbye. I thought maybe Jerry's hand on my leg was how "normal" people showed affection.

Eventually, we picked up the rest of the kids and tailgated with his family and attended the game. It was so much fun. After the game we all went back to his home to eat dinner with his family. It was great. Jerry knew how to show kids a wonderful time. It was like being in a dream family.

Nothing else weird happened until he was taking us home. He had me sit up front since I would be the last to be dropped off, and once the other kids were gone, he placed his hand back on my leg as he drove. He never once said or acted as though anything he was doing was wrong or strange in any way. That fact added to my confusion about this behavior. Was I simply over-reacting?

At age nine, I didn't know what was happening. I certainly didn't have the language even to say how it made me feel, other than the word "weird." But I overrode my instinctive feelings. I just told myself that his behavior was normal; I just wasn't used to it.

Victim Number 1, Aaron Fisher, said in his book *Silent No More* that Jerry used the exact same tactic on him: Jerry picked him up first and dropped him off last, had him sit in the front seat, and he put his hand on Aaron's leg.

Just as I did, Aaron came from a difficult family of origin. His mother was a single parent. Aaron too thought that maybe this was just the way father figures behaved in their families. He too had a weird, eerie feeling about it, but he too doubted his own instincts because of a disrupted home life. Like me, he assumed his home life was no model for the way people normally behaved.

During that football season I was asked back for more Penn State home games, and each time it was the exact same routine. I was always the first to be picked up and the last to be dropped off, and his hand was always on my leg as he drove, but only when we were alone. We would always discuss my family and school. He would tell me I was special and that I could accomplish anything I wanted. He said he wanted to help me and would if I asked him.

The following season it was the same routine, except that now his hand was higher up on my thigh and he would lightly give it a squeeze every once in a while. This is classic grooming of a child sex victim. As I said, I never even thought to say something to him about it because of the simple fact that I thought it was normal for him to act this way with people he felt close to.

An Unspoken "Deal"

Yet there was another reason I kept silent about it. Who was I to protest anything Jerry was doing? Look at what I was getting to do! I didn't want my special privileges to be taken away because of protesting or questioning Jerry's behavior. Associating with Jerry and The Second Mile were the bright spots of my life because of all the wonderful benefits he provided. I wasn't going to risk losing all that.

Sometimes in relationships we sense how things are going to be; there are unspoken "deals." I was pretty sure the unspoken deal with Jerry was that I had to "put up and shut up" about his physical approaches to me or else he would drop me.

My intuition was correct. Many guys have come forward about Jerry, describing the sexual victimization they suffered at his hands. It's been speculated that he started abusing boys as soon as he started The Second Mile (in the late 1970s) and continued doing it until his arrest in 2011. He might have started even before that. In fact, Clemente states that most preferential child sex offenders realize in late adolescence that they are sexually attracted to younger children and they begin offending shortly thereafter. That means that Jerry may have begun offending when he was still living in the home he grew up in which, conveniently, was a home in which his father, Arthur, cared for disadvantaged youth. It is very probable that there were boys there who received his criminal attentions.

Some of those who have come forward had managed to avoid Jerry's victimization, but they did pay a price for it by violating the "unspoken deal" with him. They testified that as soon as they protested verbally to Jerry about his behavior, or pushed away his hand, or ran away from him in an obvious way, they were dropped from his roster of favorite kids. There were no more privileges, no more gifts, no more favors. They were never invited again to free games and fun times. If you refused his advances, he was done with you.

This was true of Victim Number 5, according to the Grand Jury's investigative report. After Victim 5 fended Jerry off in the showers, eluded him, and went to get dry and dressed by himself, Victim Number 5 cannot recall ever being asked to another event or outing with Jerry.

It is not unusual for child victims groomed into sexual victimization to fear losing their offender's favors and attention if they speak out. They sense there is some sort of tacit bargain going on, and they go along with it to fill their hunger for adult care and love, especially those who, like many Second Milers, came from distressed, abusive, broken homes. In the parlance of child sex crimes experts, grooming creates deep ambivalence in the hearts and minds of child sex crimes victims. In other words, they have strong feelings for and against the offender. They love the attention, affection, access, and assets they are getting from the offender, while at the same time they hate the sexual activity that they are being made to endure.

Jerry would have us all shower after the game in the locker room before we went back to his house to eat. The kids would shower in the players' shower while he showered in the coaches' locker room. At least there was that separation at that time, yet this was also likely part of his grooming practices. By "letting" us shower in the players' locker room, we would become used to showering in gang showers and being naked in front of other boys and older people (i.e., the college football players). It was just one step removed from showering with Jerry himself.

Some time when I was between the ages of ten and eleven years old, Jerry started picking me up the Friday night before the home games. He would take me to the Penn State locker room and give me a pair of blue mesh PSU shorts, a gray t-shirt, and Nike sneakers. I would change into them, and then we would go work out in the weight room, or we would go to the Rec Hall to play racquetball. When we would finish working out or playing racquetball, we would head back to the locker room to shower. Before we showered we would wrestle around, just the two of us. We would take turns pinning each other; then it would be off to the showers.

He would always say, "Got to get cleaned up." The only difference was now I was in the coaches' locker room with him. It was a room that had a lock on the door with a code that needed to be entered to open the door. I was not with my friends, I was not with kids my own age. I was alone in a locked room with a grown man.

The first time I had to strip in front of him, I felt so afraid and ashamed. I tried every excuse as to why I didn't need to shower, but it was no good. He removed his clothes and I was told to and did the same, trying to keep my little boy parts covered. When we entered the shower he indicated that we should use showers right next to each other. There were small, yellowish bars of soap that we would use to wash and a specific dandruff shampoo that he supplied himself. To this day I start to gag any time I smell either of these products.

He would lather his hands up and then rub them on my head and shoulders. Here came that feeling again; that sense of being uncomfortable. That's all my little boy mind could think of: that it was uncomfortable. It wasn't fatherly; it wasn't friendly; it wasn't necessary for him to soap me up and touch me so much. I was over ten years old and perfectly capable of washing my own body and hair. It was just strange.

Also during this time he started to give me warm-up suits and sneakers from Nike and he told me I could keep them. I felt so lucky to have real clothing like normal kids wore. I didn't feel like the scruffy, poor kid I was. I had never had such nice, cool things before. I figured I would have to deal with the uncomfortable things Jerry did, because it was worth it with everything I was getting.

If you can understand all the privileges that being Jerry's special friend afforded me and how precious they were to a deprived kid like me, you can understand why I felt so strongly that I wasn't about to mess up everything just because I was uncomfortable. It seemed like a small price to pay.

Besides the material things and privileges at Penn State, I had the admiration and envy of others. Kids my age were jealous that I was hanging out with Jerry; even some adults were envious, wishing they could take my place by his side. I was his sidekick, his "Knucklehead" as he called me. That was his pet name for me.

I told Oprah Winfrey, who was a victim of child sexual victimization herself, that 90% of being with Jerry was just so stupendously great that the 10% of weirdness and discomfort seemed worth it. As a poor boy who was starved for the affection and attention of a father figure, I was totally vulnerable to Jerry and in dire need of the nurturing, love and favors he bestowed. He chose me well, and he groomed me perfectly. In time the victimization became more pronounced.

CHAPTER SIX:

The Victimization Escalates

Eventually I was asked to go to every home game and even to spend whole weekends at Jerry's house. After the games I witnessed something that was awe-inspiring to me at my young and impressionable age. I would walk back to the locker room from the stadium with Jerry, and everybody would be fighting to get next to him in order to pat him on the back and tell him what a great job he had done. He was famous; the center of attention and admiration. It was such a powerful feeling being next to him, in a favored position of access. I was no longer that miserable, bad, poor kid from Bellefonte. I was now this cool, awesome, even powerful kid who got to be side by side with Jerry Sandusky, being paraded around as his favorite. He was very protective of me too, something I had never experienced before.

As a young kid coming from where I did, I couldn't imagine anything better than what I had with Jerry. I was finally somebody, and it was all because Jerry cared about me.

On the weekend visits we would play racquetball or work out, and then I would sleep at his house. This was where some other things that Jerry did to me gave me that same weird, awkward feeling. He would always tell me I had to sleep in just my underwear or mesh shorts because a person's body needed to breathe at night. He told me I shouldn't wear anything else because it would impede that from happening. This was the second most famous coach in the United States. I figured he knew what he was talking about when it came to the human body. In fact, I thought Jerry knew everything, and I didn't ever question his logic. In hindsight, this was a now obvious ploy to give him easier access to me sexually, and it is an indicator of how advanced and well thought out his grooming skills were. Clearly, by the time he had gotten to me, Jerry had had many boys to practice and perfect these techniques on.

He would wrestle with me and blow raspberries on my stomach and make me laugh. In my kid mind I really started to feel like he was a father figure and that this was how a father treated a son he loved.

JERRY'S THREE RITUAL TIMES

As time progressed, it became clear that there were three periods of time and activities when the weirdness with Jerry occurred and started escalating. These three times were during car rides, showers, and at bedtime. The hand on my leg in the car never varied. As we spent more time together, his hand went further and further up my leg until eventually his hand was inside my shorts.

Now I know what you're thinking: just wear long pants and he can't do that. I did that, but after showering he would tell me to wear the shorts because my clothes needed washing, and his wife would wash them when we got home. It wasn't something that I could argue about. He had everything figured out and it was always his way or the highway. I wasn't going to risk upsetting him just because it made me uncomfortable. Like I said, there were just too many benefits to being Jerry's favorite for me, a young and inarticulate kid, to start rocking the boat with vague feelings that this was weird and awkward. So I endured the car ride groping.

Next were the shower room incidents. As we wrestled before each shower, he got so he was constantly putting his groin in my face while his was in mine. Also he would get me on my stomach and lay on top of me, his groin on my butt. I could feel that he was aroused, and he would just lie there for what seemed liked hours to me. I would be screaming inside, telling him to get off me, but I didn't scream or yell out loud or even say anything to him. I just endured it. In my naïve mind, I couldn't think of any explanation for it other than that he must be gay.

As time went on, when he would wrestle with me, his head would be in my groin area, and he would perform oral sex on me. Other times he would force me to do the same on him. I felt so ashamed that he was doing this to me and despite the size and power differential, I felt like I was allowing him to make me do it to him. I felt this had to stay a secret, it seemed so shameful. I felt that no one must ever know what was happening between us. I would die if this ever got out.

People would come into the locker room sometimes when Jerry was sexually assaulting me, but because the code needed to be entered, and each number pressed on the keypad sounded like the bang of a drum inside the locker room, we always had ample warning that someone was coming in, and he would stop what he was doing and act as if we were just wrestling. Sometimes the deception went to the point of Jerry asking whoever had come in to do a countdown as he pinned me.

This added another layer to Jerry's grooming and manipulations. When things like this would happen, I'd feel even more convinced that no one would believe me if I told them what he was doing to me. Jerry was simply too famous, too well known for anyone to believe that he was capable of doing such awful things to boys, and he was too powerful for anyone to do anything to stop him.

As I think back on what Jerry did to me and how he did it and where he did it, I'm sure there were people who probably knew, or at least had a glimmer of suspicion of what was going on, but because of who the perpetrator was, they probably rationalized it to themselves or else shook it off as their own wild imaginations running overtime. That happened a lot with Jerry Sandusky. People could hardly believe their own eyes when it came to him, so shining was his glory around Penn State.

The bedtime ritual, as I called it, also started to escalate in sexual contact. The raspberries on the stomach progressed downward towards my groin and inner thigh and eventually culminated in him performing oral sex on me. I call it a ritual because it was the same thing every night. At ten or eleven years old, you really don't understand what is happening. He wasn't hurting me, and, in fact, as difficult as it is to admit, it felt good physically sometimes, but it just didn't feel right.

Of course, the things he was doing had physical effects on my body, ones that I tried to will it not to have. As Oprah said, your own body betrays you in situations like these, because we are meant to respond sexually to such stimulation, even if it is at the wrong time, in the wrong circumstances, and with the wrong person. People are sexual beings—every cell in our bodies marks us as XY or XX. We're defined in every cell as being male or female, belonging to a sex. We respond to sexual stimulation with a certain amount of pleasure, even when we don't want to.

So I started to feel like I must be gay. Why else would this be happening? With my limited understanding of child sexual victimization, I felt I knew he must be gay from the things that he was doing to me. But having my body react the way it did made me think I must be gay too. It was the only language I had to decipher what was happening. I had no idea what consensual sex was like, and I didn't have the words to even try to tell anyone what was happening. I had no idea that what he was doing to me was illegal and a serious sex crime.

I also wasn't going to tell, because while what was happening was weird and uncomfortable, it was nothing compared to the pain I would receive from a beating by my grandfather or the pain of having to go to sleep hungry. I figured that if this was what I had to deal with to avoid those other sufferings, then so be it.

Other than those three types of circumstances—driving, showering, and bedtime at his home or a hotel—Jerry treated me and spoke to me as if I was his son, and that was something I had always been looking for: a father who would love me, provide for me, take care of me, make me feel like I was worthy of all of these things, and make life's road a little easier for me. Jerry was that man for me, and the weirdness just seemed like the price of admission to the wonderful life he had to offer a kid like me.

Going Again to Hawaii

As the victimization escalated, my mental ability to leave the place I was in came back to me. Once again, in my mind I would go visit Hawaii. This time I did it to escape the immense feelings of being uncomfortable, just as I had once used it to escape from the pain of my upbringing and from being beaten. Many children who are sexually victimized over a period of time use these mental escape mechanisms. I read of a little girl who would stare at the light bulb on the ceiling as the molester raped her, trying to project herself into the light, pretending she was a moth who was flying away. This mental dissociation is common in rape victims, because something is happening to their bodies that they don't want to happen and can't control, so they flee the only way they can—with their minds and hearts.

Jerry would grab me in the showers and hold me close against his naked body. He would hold my hands behind his back so that I had to lean in on his groin area. I tried to shower in a spot away from him, but he would say, "Here, I warmed this one up for you," and, of course, it would be the one right next to him.

I never told him to stop, and I never questioned him. He never acknowledged that anything he was doing was wrong. Again, as I told Oprah, I think he really had convinced himself that this was a way of showing fondness to me, that he really cared for me and that this was part of that warm affection. Like other child molesters who engage in some sort of service to children, he might have convinced himself that this was his reward for going out of his way so much for me, and it was a natural part of it. I am sure he thought he was showing some sort of love to me, and maybe that is why, to this day, he still proclaims his innocence in regard to me and all the other boys he victimized.

The sexual victimization didn't abate with time. I would travel with him alone for Second Mile events or to football conferences, and he would sexually victimization me on those trips. As I attended more and more Second Mile events, I started to get the feeling I was being shown off to others. Jerry was very possessive of me and always had me by his side. He victimized me on the campus, in hotel rooms on these trips, and also in his own home.

When we would be at his house he would always take me off by myself and speak to me. It was his way of checking in. He didn't exactly instruct me never to tell or talk about what was happening. It really wasn't necessary for him to verbalize it to me. Telling wasn't even a thought in my head.

Much has been made out of the idea that his wife Dottie must have known what was going on. I'm skeptical as to how she couldn't have known or at least sensed something, but it is possible. Although I can't answer what she did or didn't know, I do know that she walked in on things that most wives would think to be inappropriate for their husbands to be doing. Still, it is also possible that she, like so many people in the Happy Valley community, were blinded by Jerry's kindness to kids, his fame, and the respect and acclaim he enjoyed everywhere he went. It was certainly dazzling to me too, and it helped me turn a blind eye myself to what was really going on between me and the man who victimized me.

A Price Too High to Pay

Yet as time moved forward, I started to change and grow. I became less and less okay with enduring what was happening to me. I still didn't consider telling anyone. Who would have believed me anyway? There was that imbalance in power and prestige, for sure. I was a poor kid from Bellefonte. Jerry was a god. Who would take my word over his? I would just create a big stir and mess, and I would risk losing everything that I was being given. That was why I stayed silent, to Jerry and the world. Experts tell me this is a phenomenon that they see in many child sex victims, a deep ambivalence for and against the offender.

Yet I couldn't stay silent to myself. I didn't like what he was doing to me, and there was no avoiding that truth. I didn't like it. It was weird and strange. I dreaded the rides, the pre-shower wrestling matches, the shower room embraces, and the bedtime ritual when I stayed overnight. Jerry sexually assaulting me was getting to me. As time went on it was overshadowing the good times in a big way.

These are some of the complexities of child sexual victimization. The molesters give you something you want or need, and in return, they extract a price. That price is way too high to pay for any favors or benefits the molester might provide. At the time, though, the vulnerable child might not realize how terribly high that price really is, because he or she is so needy and sexuality is so dimly perceived. Over time, though, it may become clear.

A recent case in Oxfordshire, England broke wide open in the press. A gang of seven grown men enticed adolescent girls (and some boys) into sexual relationships with them and into paid sex with men they brought to the children. As in many typical child sexual victimization cases, they groomed the young girls and boys by pretending to be their friends and giving them favors of various kinds, including and especially adult attention. Once their victims were groomed into a certain amount of compliance, the men began to compel them. One girl was led into soft drugs, then alcohol, and then addiction to hard drugs. The men would supply her with the drugs she craved but she had to pay for it by acting as a prostitute for men they assigned to her. This is the way they controlled her.

It is no surprise that these predatory men actually hung out outside of the social services building to find their prey. Underprivileged kids are starved for love, care, and attention. They are easy targets and frequently unprotected by their parents. They are very vulnerable to the types of favors the molesters offer.

In one case in Oxfordshire, the young girl was enticed by the mere smile of one of the perpetrators. Apparently, in her young life with an abusive family of origin, she had rarely been smiled at. It might have been like sunshine to a maximum security prisoner—only the sunshine led to an even greater trap. Even after the men were all arrested, this victim expressed that it was hard for her to believe that the perpetrators were really bad men. They had been kind to her. They had treated her nicely, except for the sexual expectations. Can you imagine being so hungry for love that a mere smile from an adult could entice you into putting up with such things as sexual assault? That you would be willing to put up with multiple, unwanted sex partners at this person's behest in order to be smiled at? The more mentally and emotionally starved a young person is, the more willing he or she is to pay whatever price the "nice guy" offender wants.

In the end, this victim had the same ambivalent feelings about the offenders who victimized her that I had about Jerry when she remembered their smiles and kindness. His attention and favoritism had been flattering—the clothes and the money were nice too. I came to feel a mixture of love and hate in my heart toward the perpetrator.

Going along with a child sexual offender in order to receive some favors in life is truly a bargain with the devil, but a child does not know that, and cannot be expected to know that, until it is too late. There is no such thing as a consenting child. Children are developmentally too immature to make those kinds of decisions. That is why the law protects children from being taken advantage of in this way, as well as from their own bad decisions.

I was changing as I got older, though, and began to understand more about sexuality. The price was becoming too high to pay.

CHAPTER SEVEN:

Acting Out to Get Away

I *tried.*

I tried to distance myself and didn't go over to Jerry's house as often as I had in the past. Attempting to avoid his company, I would hide or leave when I knew he was coming to my house to pick me up. My mother knew I was trying to avoid him too.

Yet he came up with a new idea to keep me around. He placed me in a program that involved him giving me money as I reached goals in the program. It was a work-out program. Two Second Mile supporters were providing the funds. For Jerry, the program ensured that I would be there for him to do what he wanted with me. For me, every time I received a check that had the Second Mile logo on it, it was such a great feeling of empowerment. Jerry had upped the rewards very effectively, it was all part of his manipulative genius, and it worked on me for a time.

Soon the novelty of the money wore off, though, and my strong feelings against what I had to go through to stay in Jerry's good graces increased. It was definitely not okay. I once again started to avoid Jerry when he would come to pick me up for weekend visits. I would hide and tell my mom to tell him I wasn't there, or I would go for a sleepover at a friend's house instead of going home when I knew he was coming to pick me up.

I would later learn that several other of Jerry's victims did this when they became old enough to understand what was he was really doing to them and what his underlying motivations were: they started hiding when he came to see them or escaping to other places when he was due to arrive.

In some cases (mine included) adults in our lives couldn't understand why we didn't want to be with Jerry any more. It was a source of puzzlement to some school officials and parents.

In hindsight, this behavior should have been a huge red flag. They should have drilled down to find out what the basis of this behavior was. Instead, they left it as a curiosity. Other parents were philosophical about it, thinking it was just natural. We were getting older and we had outgrown him. Some tried to push their sons closer to Jerry because the parents had been groomed by him just as effectively as his victims had been, and they believed that Jerry's influence was really good for their children.

I don't know if there is a playbook for child sexual offenders, although NAMBLA (North American Man Boy Love Association) does publish "handbooks" on how men can "seduce" boys into sex. However, most child sex offenders figure it out through a series of trial and error experiences. They certainly seem to follow a pattern. They groom the child and they groom the child's parents or guardians and in some cases they also groom the entire community or even the country or the world. The hard-pressed single mother who worries that her son has no male role models is relieved when a Jerry Sandusky comes along. He can give her child what she can't. He takes the child off her hands for some much-needed respite so she can care for her other children or take a little time for herself. Since she is often the sole financial support of the family and probably works long hours, only to face housework, dishes, and laundry at the end of a long day, she welcomes the man into her son's life. Such a person may seem heaven-sent; plus he seems so nice; he offers such constructive and fun activities, and he's "so good with kids." The parent is groomed only a little less than the child.

The novel *Lolita* by Vladimir Nabokov is about a sexual predator interested in young girls. To have access to Lolita, the molester grooms Lolita's mother, eventually even marrying the mother to be near the child. When the mother dies, he has total access to the object of his desires, a helpless child. Eventually, though, Lolita runs off with yet another child molester. He seems to be her only avenue of escape, and finally, she escapes from him too. She grows up, marries, and has children. She builds a normal life for herself. At the end of the book, Lolita expresses to the offender the victim of child sexual victimization's very real conclusion: "You broke my life."

DRUGS AND SELF-HARM

WARNING! In this section I discuss harmful activities that I engaged in as a way of escaping the pain and isolation I experienced as a result of being sexually victimized as a child. In retrospect, I wish I had never engaged in these harmful actions and I am in no way suggesting that victims or anyone else engage in these or similar activities. Instead, anyone who is tempted to engage in self-harm should reach out to the services referenced at the end of this book. I don't want others to suffer the way that I did.

If a person can't get away from the person who is destroying his or her life, the person will try to send signals. For my part I sent signals to the world of my pain and entrapment by becoming aggressive and acting out. I got into fights and disobeyed every rule that was given to me at home and in school. In fact, it was all a wordless cry for help.

It was around this time that I started to turn to various means to block my internal pain. I couldn't speak to anyone about what was happening, so I subconsciously started looking for outlets for my frustration and wadded up feelings. I tried marijuana one day and knew that I had found what I was looking for. The feeling was amazing; it made me not care about what was happening. I experienced euphoria. Maybe for the first time in a couple of years, I didn't think about all the sexual victimization or about Jerry at all. As bad as it would turn out to be for me, I knew this was what I needed to escape.

Also, almost accidentally, I found another outlet for my pain. I found something that many kids use these days to cope with stress-filled lives. I found self-inflicted physical pain, or self-harm. It seemed to help offset the mental and emotional pain and stress in a temporary way.

As it turned out, the kids that I first got high with had a ritual for all first time smokers. We smoked the marijuana from a metal pipe, and the ritual was that once the marijuana was all smoked, the "newbie" had to heat up the bowl end of the pipe then stick it to his or her own arm. It was a branding of sorts to show that you no longer were a marijuana virgin. Since I was the newbie, I took the pipe and held a lighter up to the bowl of the pipe, much as my father had done to my toes when I was two. Once the pipe bowl was red hot, I stuck it directly onto my left bicep.

The pain was excruciating; even being high didn't cut its impact, but I held it there until the bowl was no longer hot. When I removed the bowl, a giant, circular white blister had formed. It was in that moment that I realized that burning myself was a release from the stress and inner anguish I was feeling.

A lot of young people hurt themselves for the release it gives them. Cutting is a big activity, especially among young girls. For me, it was burning. Without realizing how self-destructive it was, I would spend the next few years burning myself with any metal object I could find. Sometimes I just used the metal head of the lighter I had. Somehow, the external pain served to extinguish my internal pain. It felt as though I was a balloon, and as time went on, the air inside would fill up, stretching me too thin. When it came to a point in time when I needed to release it because the pressure was just too great, I would burn myself. In essence, this was like deflating the balloon.

Self-harm allowed me to take more pressure in life without saying a single word to anyone. I would use these two things—getting high and burning myself—to survive the coming years. I was a pressure cooker, and these things were the only steam valves I could find to let some of the tension out. I only wish I had known about MaleSurvivor.org or any of the other services available to victims like me at the time. If I had, maybe I could have avoided those years of torment and self-harm.

STALKING

Once I figured out how to evade him, Jerry started stalking me. He always found ways to get to me, no matter what I did to get away or to avoid him. He would come to my school and have the guidance counselor call me in to his office to talk. I would go the office, wondering what it was about, and Jerry would be there. I would be stuck in the room alone with him, as the counselor would step out. Everyone was trying to push me closer to Jerry because they thought I needed his help. No one took the time or had the insight to realize that Jerry was actually the problem. It was easier to label me a troubled kid from a poor, broken home rather than invest the energy and emotion to figure out what was really happening. For my part, I figured it was their job to create an atmosphere of safety and trust for me to tell them the truth. They were the adults. Yet they didn't. No one even questioned whether Jerry's influence was good for me or not. They certainly never questioned me about it. I don't know if I would have told them the truth if they had asked, but I do know they didn't even bother to try.

Eventually, I turned to getting stoned every day and skipping school. That was my way to cope and escape. When I was high I didn't care about school or getting in trouble for not attending. I didn't care about Jerry and what he did to me or that the guidance counselor and every responsible adult I knew thought Jerry was a great mentor, a great benefit for my life. The truth was, he was destroying my life.

Victim Number 1, Aaron Fisher, noted in his book *Silent No More* that Jerry came to his school too, getting him out of class even against school rules. Because he was Jerry Sandusky, the rules were bent for him. The principal would call Aaron out of class, who would sometimes go hide in the bathroom rather than being forced to see Jerry. It happened so often, Aaron started getting a reputation as a bad kid, because only bad kids were called to the principal's office so often. Jerry followed Aaron's school bus home too, using the bus lane that was illegal for cars to be in. He followed Aaron to a friend's, pulled up next to him on the road, and demanded to talk to him. After a while, Jerry was screaming. He followed Aaron home and had a screaming fit on Aaron's lawn, in front of Aaron's mother and grandfather. This was brought about because Aaron was doing everything he could to disentangle his life from Jerry and Jerry was infuriated over it.

The classic stalker reaction is, the more the victims pull away, the angrier and more persistent the stalker gets. School officials and parents looked the other way when Jerry went off on their kids in the schoolyard or out in public. Adults figured Jerry was just holding the kids accountable, the way a good mentor should. They never realized that Jerry was having the classic stalker's reaction of fury when the object of their desire decides enough is enough and wants to cease all contact.

To give you an idea of how persistent Jerry could be in trying to stay close to his victims, the Grand Jury's investigative report about Jerry's activities notes that Jerry made over one hundred phone calls to one victim's cell phone and home phone combined over a seven month period, with the victim making no calls to Jerry at all. Taken in context, that's stalking behavior.

Steven Turchetta, an assistant high school principal and football coach at Clinton High School, where Aaron Fisher attended school, said in his grand jury testimony that Jerry Sandusky volunteered as an assistant football coach at the school. In fact he worked at this volunteer coaching position full time in 2008. Second Mile students were often called out of class late in the day. Turchetta said that Jerry was extremely "controlling" and that there were frequently shouting matches and that Sandusky became "clingy" and "needy" when a young man wanted to break off the relationship with him. Turchetta thought it odd at the time, even suspicious.[5]

CNN reported that in letters to Victim Number 4, while Jerry sometimes spoke as a mentor should, encouraging, advising, coaching, he also sometimes appeared to be "needy, scolding and manipulative." In fact, they reported, "At times, he sounded

5 This is from the Grand Jury's Report on its investigation of Gerald A. Sandusky.

like a love-struck teenager weathering that first painful break-up."6 Since Jerry's behavior was not consistent with what a mentor should be doing and he was acting like a jilted lover. It seems that someone in authority should have recognized the difference. Someone in authority should have stepped in to protect Aaron and to protect me, but no one did.

Offenders really do not like their victims to try to get out of the relationship. It is a sad fact that women who are being stalked by abusive husbands often wind up murdered by the spouse, the restraining orders they had gotten against their husbands folded up in their purses. Some studies have shown that half of victims of offenders are revictimized by the same person even after getting a restraining order requiring the person to stay a certain amount of feet away from them. The stalkers ignore all warnings to keep their distance. Almost 20% of victims of domestic violence who wind up murdered by perpetrators had restraining orders against those offenders and were taking steps to get away, stay away, and to keep those very offenders at bay.

Offenders don't like to be thwarted. They are too self-centered to take "no" for an answer, and they tend to think of their victims as belonging to them, having no separate existence with legal and personal rights.

When we, his victims, tried to get away from him, Jerry Sandusky stalked us, showing up at our homes and our schools, wheedling our parents and teachers into believing that he only meant us good. Many adults colluded with him, unknowingly enabling his crimes against us.

Predatory sexual stalking is nothing new. A recent movie starring Daniel Radcliffe (of *Harry Potter* fame) covers a little known incident in the lives of several members of the "Beat" generation (writers Allen Ginsberg, William S. Burroughs, Jack Kerouac, Lucian Carr, and others). The movie is entitled *Kill Your Darlings*, which is classic advice to young writers—you have

6 Ann O'Niell, CNN, "Sandusky's son fits pattern of other alleged victims." June 23, 2012. Available online at http://www.cnn.com/2012/06/22/justice/pennsylvania-sandusky-letters/index.html#.

to kill some of your finest prose if it doesn't advance your story. But the killing in this case became a literal one. One of these men—Lucien Carr—actually committed a murder one night in Riverside Park. He murdered his sexual stalker.

David Kammerer, a sexual predator who had been stalking Carr for five years, from the time Carr was fourteen years old, finally went too far, and Carr exploded. The famous Jack Kerouac was arrested when he helped Carr lose the knife with which he killed his predator.

Carr went to the police the next day and confessed to stabbing David Kammerer twice in the chest. Carr had also tied up Kammerer's body and dumped it in the Hudson River.

The reason for the killing was that David Kammerer had sexually stalked Carr all throughout Carr's adolescence to the point that Carr's parents had moved him from school to school and state to state, trying to elude Kammerer, but the stalker would not be shaken off. Eventually, in frustration at not being able to rid himself of Kammerer and his sexual advances, Carr killed him. Due to these factors, Carr only served two years in a reform school for taking the life of his predatory stalker.

As is so often the case, the stalker in that case was a leader of a youth group with altruistic purposes, namely the Boy Scouts, and that is how he met his victim. In commenting on the movie, Carr's son Caleb says it is no coincidence that Carr at last stabbed Kammerer with a Boy Scout knife. The Boy Scouts was Kammerer's hunting ground. In Carr's mind, the Boy Scouts was where the predatory sexual stalking began.

Just as it is no coincidence that Kammerer was murdered with a Boy Scout knife, it is probably not a coincidence that Kammerer was murdered just as Carr had attempted to ship out with the Merchant Marines. Kammerer no doubt stepped up his approaches toward Carr as the predator imagined losing his prey. Like Jerry, this mid-century sexual stalker did not like the idea of Carr having an existence separate from him. As Kammerer became more persistent, driven by fear of the loss of Carr, it got out of hand, and a harassed Lucien Carr finally had had enough.

Usually it is the other way around. When a victim of sex crimes tries to get away, an offender can become overbearing, even violent and desperate, the way Jerry got when a victim tried to pull away from him. The fact is, Jerry went ballistic as his child victims, evolving into teenagers with more certain sexual identities, wanted him permanently out of their lives.

A HIDING PLACE

I would skip school to avoid Jerry stalking me there. I found a place to go that was great. My hiding place was weatherproof. No matter what storms and cold were outside, I would be okay; protected from the elements. This hiding place was really good; nobody had any idea I was there. I didn't care that I was missing school or getting a reputation as a bad kid, because my hiding place meant I no longer had to see the perpetrator. It could all finally be over.

Unfortunately, my victory was short-lived. It seems that fate had other plans for what was going to happen to me. I made a major mistake where my life would be forever changed yet again; my hiding place led to another fork in the road that seemed to lead—as most of the forks in the road of my life had seemed to lead—right back to Jerry.

CHAPTER EIGHT:

Dying to Get Out

My secret location was an old barn. I used to go there with my cousin, and we would get high together. One day while skipping school and getting high there, my cousin and I made a silly blunder that would haunt us for years to come.

There was a truck in the barn, and it was a cold November morning. We didn't have the keys to start the truck, but we could get in through the unlocked doors. Inside the cab it was quite warm. I really thought my hiding spot was perfect because of this protection from the weather.

We decided to pass the hours of the school day by getting wasted. On this day we accomplished our goal of getting pretty high, and then for some dumb reason, probably because we were kids, we decided to light pieces of paper on fire. We would light a piece of paper on fire and then throw it in the glove box and slam the compartment door to extinguish the flame. It was funny, goofy—and stupid. The paper didn't extinguish in the glove compartment very well. In fact, air found its way to the burning paper, and it ignited the other papers in the glove compartment.

Before we knew what was happening, there was thick dark smoke billowing out of every vent in the truck. We were gagging and choking from the smoke, and we jumped out of the truck. We tried to climb back in and put the fire out, but it was no use. The smoke was too blinding, and the fire was growing and spreading quickly. We did what any two scared, stoned kids might do. We ran back to school, leaving the problem behind us, and pretended that we'd been there all day. We hoped the fire would miraculously be taken care of.

We were badly shaken when we learned later that everything in the barn and the barn itself caught fire. The structure burned to the ground in a huge conflagration. Of course, we had no idea of the monetary damage we had caused to someone's private property. We'd never meant to do that. We'd just been goofing around. The results astounded and terrified us.

When I heard about the building burning down, I knew I had made a terrible mistake. I was hoping against hope that they wouldn't trace the fire to me, but in my heart I knew that it was only a matter of time before the police would be showing up at my door. Sure enough, they arrived a few days later and I was told that if I just confessed to them what had happened, I would not be arrested.

I broke down and spilled my guts. I felt horrible and I had never meant for it to happen. I had never anticipated so much destruction could follow some stupid goofing around. It was an accident, but I was going to suffer the consequences for it. In spite of their promises not to arrest me, I left my mother's home in handcuffs and would never return.

I was fifteen at the time of my arrest. Hundreds of thousands of dollars of damage had been done to the property, and I was looking at about six felony charges. I tell you this not because I'm bragging about what a bad ass kid I was—not at all. I'm saying it to show you the seriousness of what I was up against when I was arrested, because this factored into my future relationship with Jerry. This is what really trapped me into dependency upon him and sealed my lips more strongly than ever before about what Jerry had done to me over the years.

Jerry to the "Rescue"

This was my first major run-in with the law. I was placed in the Centre Counties Youth Center, a juvenile detention center in Bellefonte, and I was shivering with fear over what my fate was going to be. I was assigned a public defender because my mother couldn't afford a private lawyer. It soon became clear to me that I was going to be incarcerated for a long time. I was terrified as to what lay ahead.

The youth detention center wasn't so bad. We were given three square meals a day, and there was TV and a gym. I had my own room with a window and a halfway decent bed.

One day after I'd been there about a month, I received a surprise visit from a good friend of Jerry's, Tim Janocko, who had played football for Penn State. That was really odd since I hadn't spoken to Jerry in months, and it seemed like there was no way he could have known I was in a detention center. This friend of Jerry's told me that Jerry was in California for the Rose Bowl game, but that the friend had been commissioned to come ask me if I would like to live with Jerry if Jerry could make it happen. The alternative was a military-like boot camp in Pittsburgh until I turned eighteen and then to serve time in jail for my crimes.

Of course, given the circumstances, I chose to live with Jerry. Enduring all that he would do to me while being free was way more enticing than being stuck in a boot camp and then going to jail or some other place of incarceration for who knows how long. I was in big trouble with the law, but Jerry had enough pull to be able to extricate me out of the troubles. I had seen him work his magic before. I knew he had influence and power. The price of his using it to help me was living at his house and never being able to hide from him again.

Jerry did make it happen, as only he could. I was placed in his home and was assigned a probation officer. The day I was released to his custody is a day I will never forget.

No Way Out

He took me for lunch at McDonald's and then to the locker room to work out. You would have thought that not seeing each other for months had never happened because he jumped right back into where he had left off. Jerry resumed all the same victimization as before; only one thing had changed now: he had the leverage of the police to threaten me with. I was trapped more than ever before. He would tell me that if I stepped out of line, I would be taken away to prison and there would be nothing he could do to stop it. It was something I understood right away. Now he had even more authority and control over me and could do whatever he liked to me. He knew for certain I would never tell anyone about it. Who would believe me anyway, at that stage? I was now officially a seriously "bad kid." If I reported on Jerry, it would be seen as lies and as my fault, and I would be spending a long time in prison.

Pennsylvania stands near the top of the country—and the world—in the number of juveniles who are tried as adults for serious crimes and incarcerated in regular prisons. It is not a lenient state. My future, without Jerry's influence, was bleak.

Yet after a year in his custody and a year more of enduring his sexual assaults, I couldn't take it anymore. I had to find a way out. I was starting to think that even prison wasn't such a bad idea if I could get away from what Jerry was continually doing to me.

Yet my lips were still sealed. I knew that I would never tell on Jerry. But I started to "tell" and protest in other ways.

I had to meet with my probation officer once a month and was drug tested each time. I formulated a plan to get some weed and get high and fail the test so that some kind of legal action would come in and stop the sexual assaults. I smoked up but was caught by Jerry's wife. Jerry and Dottie then took me to the hospital and had me drug tested themselves. When the test came back positive, Jerry told me that he was going to have to inform my probation officer. I was told that they contacted my probation officer and notified him that I had failed a drug test. I am not sure how the conversation went, or if it took place at all, but I know the outcome. Nothing happened and I remained in the Sandusky home.

My probation officer never spoke to me about the incident. Jerry had shown me once again that he was more powerful than the law. I had absolutely no way out.

Seeking the Release of Death

I started to have dreams about dying. I would go to sleep, and then, much like in the movies or those stories about life after life, my spirit would lift up from my body and I would spend nights just looking at myself as I lay in the bed asleep. They seemed like out-of-body experiences, and I wonder if they were a more spiritual form of "going to Hawaii"; that is, of mentally escaping from life when what was happening was just too much for my mind and spirit to bear. A very peaceful feeling always came over me during these experiences. I was not afraid to die. I actually started to believe that in death at least I would be safe and finally separated from the perpetrator.

I became fearless of death and almost begged it to take me. I would drink or get high, then hop in my car and see how fast I could go down the highway. I became very reckless and started to get into fights with kids at school with no thought for my own well-being. It wasn't that I thought I was tough and just wanted to beat people up; it was that pain and suffering became my norm. Fighting, like burning myself, became a release for me. I could take out my frustrations by using my fists.

In the movie *Fight Club* with Brad Pitt and Edward Norton, the main character (Edward Norton) discovers what a release it is to fight other men. He and Brad Pitt discover that lots of men are interested in taking out their frustrations in life through getting into fights; that's why and how they start the Fight Club. Edward Norton's character finds himself going to work on Monday and thinking of nothing but the next weekend, when he can fight again to release the pressures of modern life in this simple, primal way. I understand this feeling. Fighting was a release for me too.

I've mentioned that young people these days cut and burn themselves for stress release in what psychologists call self-harm, self-mutilation and other names. Psychologists know that this unhealthy and destructive way of coping with stress really does provide temporary relief from stress and frustration. It works in its own way, and seems very effective to a troubled young person, but is actually more damaging than the reason for doing the behavior. I know now that there are many more healthy ways to cope with frustration and stress; but I didn't know any other ways then, and many teenagers don't find healthy ways of coping with pressure. They are not that wise and resourceful. They often use destructive and self-destructive means.

Physical pain is used as a distraction from the horrific mental and emotional anguish the victim feels day by day, especially as a victim of child sexual victimization.   Self-harm and injuring and being injured in fights only goes so far in reducing stress and pain, plus it can lead to more severe problems or even death. It is no solution, and adults who suspect young people are engaging in self-harm should intervene.

In my case, I was already "dissociated" from myself mentally and physically. As a result, I started to feel like a hollow shell walking through life. On the outside I portrayed everything that everyone expected to see, but on the inside I was empty. Nobody truly knew who I was or what I was going through. I can't imagine how much better my adolescence and young adult life would have been if I had known there were so many other boys who'd gone through what I'd gone through or if I'd had access to a professional therapist trained in providing counseling to boys who'd been sexually victimized. Instead of being able to get help to deal with the crimes that were committed against me, I suffered in painful silence.

Eventually, I decided that the peaceful dreams of being out of my body were a calling. It was my time to leave this plane of existence and travel to the next, where I would no longer feel grief and strain. If the Sunday school and church teachings where correct, then there was a paradise waiting for me, and if by chance it wasn't true and all that happened was that the lights went out one last time, I would be okay either way. Death seemed like the ultimate escape from anguish, and it was time to work up the courage to go for it.

In March of 1996, I finally summoned the courage to end my own life. I thought that was the only way for me to escape, and I couldn't wait any longer.

I was in a relationship with a girl, and late one night we sneaked out of the house and made a pact to end our lives. I am not sure what made her decide to do it. We never talked about why, just how. We bought two large bottles of aspirin and started swallowing them by the hundreds. We waited a bit and when nothing seemed to be happening, we decided to try the hose-in-the-tailpipe way—breathing in poisonous carbon monoxide from a car. While we were trying it, though, the girl got violently ill, and I realized I didn't want her to die. I made the decision to drive her to the hospital.

To this day I do not remember the drive there. I only remember telling the ER people what had happened to her and then returning to the waiting room where I blacked out on the floor. I wanted to save her, but I still wanted to die myself.

It wasn't to be, though. They admitted me to the hospital and started pumping my stomach. I had to drink liquid charcoal that soaked up the toxins in my stomach. It made me vomit uncontrollably.

As I look back, I realize that to my adolescent mind it seemed like the perfect plan. I could take my life and nobody would see why I had done it. They would say it was two dumb kids with a Romeo and Juliet complex. It would never have been thought that I took my life because a man that the entire world worshiped, it seemed, was sexually abusing me.

I was eventually moved from the ER once I was stable enough and transferred to a normal room. To add insult to injury, Jerry was notified of what had happened. I will never forget the moment I saw him walk through the door of my room. You would think he would be concerned about my health or why I did it, but he wasn't. He had a big smile on his face. He simply said, "You can't even kill yourself right" and then laughed. There was no escaping that man or his ways of demeaning me.

As I look back on this now, I see it for what it was, one more level of control over me. Even at the lowest point in my life, when I had clearly made a real effort to end my own life, Jerry could not pass up an opportunity to undercut my self-esteem. He was making me feel even more helpless than I already did in the hopes that it would drive me closer to him. He wanted me to feel so helpless and lost on my own that I couldn't possibly survive without him. The thing is, that I obviously was way beyond that point, because I didn't even want to survive.

Since I didn't end up dying, I was subjected to a lot of therapy, but I still didn't disclose the real cause of my anguish. I told them the reason I had done it was because of a girl. Everyone bought it and nobody really tried to dig deeper to find out what was really there. The victimization that I had been suffering at the hands of Jerry Sandusky was the true cause of me trying to end my life. Enduring that for years on end left me feeling I had nothing left to live for.

Even though I stayed in the psych ward at the hospital for a week and underwent intense therapy, not once did I even think about telling the counselor the real reason why I had tried to take my own life. Besides the complexities of disclosure, which I will go into in further chapters, I never trusted therapists. That mistrust started when I was seeing a therapist at The Second Mile. We would have meetings where I would speak generally about life, never going really deep, and he would then tell Jerry everything I said. Jerry would sit me down and lecture me about whatever I might have said that he had an issue with. I knew it was not safe to trust a therapist not to betray me to Jerry, and that formed my thought processes about therapy for years to come.

I was eventually released back into Jerry's care and home. You would think that after attempting suicide while in foster care and on probation, there would have been a few agencies looking closely at my placement back into that home, but there were none. No one seemed to question whether that placement was good for me or not. I wonder how some of the people responsible thought about it (if they did think about it) after Jerry was indicted and convicted of all those counts of child sexual victimization. Did anyone regret that they did not look into my case more closely? I hope so. I hope there was some regret and self-examination, because too many kids in foster care fall through the cracks.

In fact, Jerry had me write a letter to my probation officer apologizing for what I had done and saying I was a bad kid and that being with the Sandusky's was where I wanted to be. I took responsibility for everything that I had done. My probation officer accepted it and that was the end of it. Child and Youth Services had a case worker come by and meet with me, only I wasn't there at the time, and they took Dottie's word for it that I was okay and that no further action was needed. Case closed.

THE CONTROLLER

What this reinforced for me was that I was trapped. There was no way out and this man controlled everything in my life and he always would. It was made very clear to me that I would never be encouraged to speak about what had happened to me at the hands of Jerry Sandusky by anyone who had any authority to stop the victimization.

My suicide attempt did have one good outcome. The overtly sexual victimization stopped. I was never sexually assaulted again after that day. I can only guess as to why Jerry stopped his most severe sexual assaults against me at this time. Was it because I finally grew out of the age range of the perpetrator, or could it have been because I was now bringing a lot of attention to myself and, by association, to the perpetrator and his behaviors? Did he fear that I was so much on the brink psychologically that disclosure was an ever-present danger for him? Did he dimly realize on an unconscious level that his behavior toward me was making me deeply troubled—troubled enough to try to do away with myself? I don't know. The evidence suggests that by this time he was most likely grooming and victimizing other boys already, turning his attention away from me to them. Experts refer this to as "the grooming pipeline," a manifestation of the fact that child sex offenders can never "couple for life" with their victims. Children always "age-out" of the desired age range that the offenders are attracted to. Therefore, offenders develop a pattern of behavior that allows them to get continued access to new potential victims over time. They can actually be grooming multiple children at the same time while offending against them consecutively. They can also be offending against two or more of them concurrently.

Despite the fact that Jerry ceased the worst of his crimes against me, he would always pull me away from the rest of the family and remind me of what would happen if I ever spoke about what he had done to me. He would pull me into a bedroom and tell me how probation or the police had spoken to him and that he was able to smooth everything over. They were always trying to take me away to jail but he believed in me and would fight for me as long as I was fighting for the family. He would always be reminding me of how the family stood by me through all of my troubles and how it was my turn to do the same for them. I assured him I never would. This behavior on Jerry's part makes me think that the real reason Jerry decided to stay away from me sexually was not because he realized how much pain he was causing to another human being; not just because he was ready to move on to younger and easier prey. It was very likely because my suicide attempt brought me into contact with therapists and authorities, and he feared I was going to disclose and I might bring down the façade of his altruistic public persona, exposing the manipulative, perverted child sex offender that Jerry really was.

Now Jerry started talking to me about being adopted into his family. The reasoning that he explained to me made a lot of sense at the time. Jerry told me that I would be attending Penn State and that I had to pay for my own tuition and books. If I had the Sandusky last name, I would get a huge break on tuition and only pay a quarter of the full price. Of course, I look back on this situation now and I know that this was just one more level of Jerry's grooming me and the community. By offering to adopt me, he would maintain authority and control over me legally. He would constantly be able to measure his level of effectiveness of that control. He would also show to the community that he was an altruistic man, and he would make it even harder for me to disclose, because he knew everyone would question why I had agreed to be adopted by a man who had sexually assaulted me over a number of years. In short, this was a strategy move as or more brilliant than any Jerry devised and implemented on the football field. It locked me in to another decade-plus of silence, while it ensured his ability to go on grooming and sexually assaulting other boys.

The adoption was an easy decision for me. I had already been associated with the family; I would attain even more social and "political" power by bearing the name; there was no escaping this man and his wishes anyway; and college would be cheaper. College might not even be possible without this strategy move, and it might just be the ultimate way out.

The only issue obstructing Jerry was that my biological mother would not let the adoption go through. She fought as hard as she could to remain my legal mother, but eventually I turned eighteen and it was no longer her decision.

I was taken to the chambers of a Centre County judge, the same judge who had placed me in foster care with the Sandusky family. He asked me some basic questions and whether this is what I wanted. I said yes and it was over and done with. I went into the meeting as Matthew Heichel and I left Matthew Sandusky. There was no formal hearing in a courtroom and no opportunity for anyone to give reasons as to why this wasn't a good idea. It was what Jerry wanted to happen and so it happened, period. He had the kind of pull that makes things happen easily, and I went along with him because it made sense for my future.

Of course what I didn't think about at the time was that by this time Jerry had adopted a number of boys (the number would eventually reach five boys and one girl "for Dottie") so he was an old hand at this process. These adoptions, certified by the judicial process, would cumulatively add to his status and standing in the community, and they would give him and even greater opportunity to groom and molest other boys.

Of course, the adoption meant that when I started college, I was forced to live at Jerry's home, yet another level of continued control. Jerry would explain to me that probation would not allow me to live on campus (to this day I have no idea if that was true). I had to be home for dinner every night, and he would make me study. I would also have to meet him at the locker room during the day to work out or go play some sport, sometimes with younger Second Mile kids. He retained power over my bank account so I could not withdraw money or have a credit card. I was given a weekly allowance and when I spent that, I eventually turned to stealing money from my adopted mother's purse. I would take a $20 bill every once in awhile. It was wrong and I acknowledge that. I also understand that it may not make me look like that great of a person, but in the interests of justice I promised to tell the truth here. So I am fully disclosing everything, despite the fact that at times it may be against my personal interests.

Why did I steal? I'd like to explain because I want people to see that these types of behaviors have some reasoning behind them, no matter how faulty. These kinds of behaviors should be a "red flag" that can clue family, friends, teachers, administrators, child care workers, psychologists, police officers and judges in to the fact that there is some underlying anomaly in a child's life that they need to address. I didn't take the money just to take it. I took it because the man who was victimizing me controlled every aspect of my life. I was only allowed to have what he allowed me to have, when he allowed me to have it. Stealing was an expression of defiance and felt like a little bit of freedom.

That's the only way I can explain it. No matter where I went or what happened, Jerry Sandusky controlled my life. I was trapped and still dying to get out, and stealing allowed me to break that control in small measure.

Yet, as I mentioned, my failed suicide attempt actually marked a turning point in my life. Jerry never victimized me again after my attempt on my own life. It took that much for him to stop sexually assaulting me, but I think he stopped more to protect himself than he did to protect me.

CHAPTER NINE:

It's Complicated

I lived in the Sandusky home until I was twenty-one, which was when my probation ended. I left as soon as I could and Jerry was not happy about that. Again, he stalked me and came by my place often. Even though I never gave him the address, somehow he found it, and he threatened to call the police on me for stealing things that I hadn't stolen. I suspect that some may think, "Okay, if you didn't steal anything, then why be worried?" Well, as I mentioned, I had stolen sometimes from his family, so he did have that on me from the past. What was more, Jerry could make things happen. He'd proven time and again that his threats were very real. He was able to get me out of a detention center, have an adoption rubber-stamped by a judge, and even arrange things so that my suicide attempt triggered no serious investigation. I had been brainwashed to believe that I was a bad kid and that I was destined for prison. Because I had a history of stealing, Jerry convinced me that he was the only one able to stop me from going to prison; he was my savior, and from where I stood, I could see he did have tremendous pull in the community. So I felt I had to endure Jerry's continuing to be a part of my life.

I wonder now if he was fearful that if he didn't keep me close, I might disclose his crimes to someone. I don't know for sure, but it certainly seems that way. All I know is that my mind had been shaped by victimization as a child, and I wasn't able to comprehend a lot of things people comprehend as adults. I eventually moved back into the Sandusky home because it was just easier than dealing with his constant threats as I tried to pull away from him.

Eventually, I married and had three beautiful children. I did not spend much time around the Sandusky family during that

marriage, and it drove Jerry insane. He would constantly be calling and trying to get me to come over to his house. He would
come by our home unannounced and ask to speak with me. This
was different from his previous stalking behavior. Now he was
always trying to make sure our secret was safe and that I knew
the consequences if it wasn't.

During this period of time it was more nonverbal than verbal. By showing up unannounced at places where he shouldn't
even be able to find me, let me know that he was in control. He
was most likely checking in to see if my wife would say anything
to him about the sexual abuse. He was looking for any sign that
I had disclosed to anyone. He maintained the fear of him that he
had instilled in me from an early age. I told him many times: he
had nothing to fear; my lips were sealed, forever.

After eight years my wife and I divorced. I had nowhere to
go at that time, and I had to once again move back into the
Sandusky home. This would be another turning point in my life.

Why Victims Go Back

People will ask, "If you were victimized by him, why would
you go back there?" Some people use this reasoning to assert
that I must be lying about the crimes Jerry committed against
me, because I walked back into the home of the offender of my
own free will. There are several reasons why I did that. For one
thing, the victimization had stopped by that time, and I was an
adult. That meant that I was better prepared to defend myself in
the event Jerry tried to assault me again, but it also meant that he
was no longer interested in me sexually. For another, it is important to understand how complicated the issue of victimization,
especially child sexual victimization, really is.

To people who have never experienced any kind of victimization, it must be genuinely puzzling why a victim would ever
return to a perpetrator. Yet very often victims have mixed feelings about the offenders who committed crimes against them.
Survivors of childhood sexual victimization may feel a mixture

of disgust and confusion toward their offenders, but they may also feel a certain amount of affection and protectiveness toward them, even gratitude for the kindnesses the offender has shown them. This is particularly true of a parent/child-type bond.

Children of abusive parents are often deeply bonded with their parents in spite of the victimization. They beg not to be separated from their parents because, no matter how dysfunctional or destructive, they cling to the only family they know. The bond between Jerry and me resembled a parent/child bond, at least from my side of things. I was certainly not emotionally free of him, and I was not entirely without affection toward him. I know this must be very difficult for people to understand, but despite all of the crimes Jerry committed against me, he saved me from a father who was even more violently abusive to me than Jerry was. He saved me from a life that I had been conditioned to believe was destined for disaster without him. He gave me what I considered at the time was an opportunity to be part of a real, prominent, and prosperous family. Those are things I needed to survive. Those are things that I still cling to as the building blocks of the life I have now built for myself. In fact, the ability to surgically excise the horrible things Jerry did to me from the good that he provided me, despite the clearly perverted motive behind all of it, was a critical component of my survival and healing process.

There have been cases in which law enforcement officials have seen the return of a survivor to the person who molested them as proof that the survivor is lying about the crimes. Yet that's not true. In Dr. Susan Weitzman's book on upscale women in abusive marriages, *Not to People Like Us*, she noted how very long many of the survivors stayed with their offenders or returned to them after an escape attempt. Some waited to make a permanent departure only after the victimization had caused permanent injury. Some could only bring themselves to turn their lives upside down by leaving forever when they thought their children were in danger.

Although law enforcement may at times look at a survivor's willingness to return to a person and place of victimization or to stay in a relationship as a reason to believe the person is lying about the victimization, in fact, that behavior is more "normal" (that is, usual) than "abnormal" (that is, unusual). However difficult it is for outsiders to understand, it is very common for a victimized person to remain in contact with the offender, sometimes very close contact indeed.

Why? Offenders are people we know. They are rarely strangers. Often, they are people who are woven closely into the fabric of our lives. We have formed bonds with them. Bonds bind, whether those bonds are healthy, unhealthy or mixtures of both.

Let's face it: relationships and the human beings within them are complex, even (and maybe especially) within abusive relationships. Very few relationships are cut and dried; easily pigeon-holed and explained. Victims may not achieve real clarity about the victimization they suffered for many, many years. They may perceive somehow that the victimization was their doing, their fault, that they brought it on themselves. Certainly a lot of offenders reinforce that kind of thinking in their victims. This dynamic adds to the victim's confusion and the unwillingness to sever all ties with the offender.

In my case, I had been treated from a young age as if I was a "bad" kid. I had a damaged self-image. I believed that what was happening to me was my fault and that I somehow deserved it. I thought that a kid like me had to pay a heavy price to enjoy the benefits of being favored by the influential, trusted, and loved Jerry Sandusky.

As I grew older that image didn't change much. It was deeply rooted, and up until a couple of years ago, it was something I believed to be as true as I believe the sky is blue. I did not trust myself, and I figured no one else trusted me either. I know that if I had told my biological family what had happened to me, even they would have thought I was lying. If I told anyone about what Jerry Sandusky had done to me and forced me to do, I would be kicked out of the Sandusky family, and I had some deep bonds among those family members too. I've mentioned that I told Oprah that life with the Sanduskys was 90% great. It really was. There were lots of kids around, plenty of activities, food, and fun. That might not seem like much, but to a kid who was born into a dirt-poor, abusive family, they were paradise in comparison. There were also sports and sports facilities and gear, things that any boy would love to have access to. In short, there was wealth and all that money could buy.

The Sandusky's life was an extremely kid-friendly one. They were unable to have biological children of their own, due in part to an old football injury, as Jerry explained to me one time, although I now wonder if this was just one more manipulation by Jerry. Did he get married to Dottie and feign the inability to father children so he could convince her to adopt? Did he marry her specifically because she couldn't conceive? Did he simply use this as an excuse to not have sex with her? All these were possibilities running through my head at the time, based on all the lies he had told me to build the facade of who he truly was. Whatever way it happened, the Sanduskys had adopted a total of six children and fostered many others. They had received an "Angels in Adoption" award. They had always surrounded themselves with children, and they knew what kids liked.

I often think about and have been asked many times about Dottie's role in all of this. Why did she find it so easy to turn on me, without ever having one conversation with me, and unconditionally support Jerry? To forsake my safety and welfare, her adopted child, I ask myself is this reaction possible evidence of her complicity in all of this? These thoughts occur to me today as possibilities. I will never be sure, but I do believe, at a minimum, it is proof positive of her unabashed denial.

Having lived with the Sandusky family for years, I felt I was a part of the family. I felt loved by all of the Sandusky family members, and I had love for all of them. This includes the offender. I loved the man who perpetrated against me as my father even as I hated him for abusing me.

People want to believe that child sexual victimization is a black and white issue. It most certainly is not. Perhaps more than any other form of abusive relationship, sexually abusive relationships with children are the most complex. Certainly I have found in my life experiences that this issue has a large swath of gray area. There is a great deal of ambivalence; there is anger mingled with loyalty. There is the strong and burning desire for the love the offender gives and hatred that the love is polluted by the crimes the offender commits.

There is also the factor that when a perpetrator has spent years grooming you, it totally messes up your head. The lines between right and wrong are blurry, not clear. Boundaries have been broken when the child is developmentally immature, and as a result the child doesn't even know what boundaries are or what they should be. Guilt and shame play a significant role as well. As they say, it is complicated.

To understand this, just imagine for a moment how it feels to get into a serious argument with a loved one. Afterward the love and the anger are all mixed up with extreme emotion, pain, and confusion, so much so, that you are not sure who was right and who was wrong. You don't remember who said the first sharp remark or what caused it all to escalate the way it did. Try as you might, you can't get into the other person's mind to understand his or her thinking, and you know your own thoughts and feelings weren't understood. You are hurt by the very one you love and you have hurt the very one you love. You feel both violated and guilty. If this happens often, the relationship can become more and more unclear and painful, more and more of a morass that may need professional help to be sorted out.

If even normal relationships can be this complicated, imagine how complicated abnormal relationships are. I can testify to the fact that when it comes to the relationship between an offender and his or her child victim, a relationship that is not at all normal, the complications multiply. The child doesn't know who is insane—the perpetrator, who seems to think everything is just fine and who may be in total denial, or you, who knows what is going on underneath all the sugar coating and is freaking out inside. Offenders can be very manipulative and controlling; they can convince or coerce you into thinking that you are the one at fault.

These are just some of the reasons so many victims not only do not walk away from abusive relationships, if they ever do get free, they walk right back into them. Some never walk out at all; they stay in abusive relationships for years or decades. With all the complications going on, the ensuing silence of victims of child sex crimes can be deafening.

Going Numb

I loved the times when Jerry was caring for me like a father and we were all together as a family. It was all that I hungered for; in some ways, it was what I lived for.

Yet I hated it that his insidious victimization had such a profound effect on the way I felt in this world. During the times Jerry victimized me, I would dissociate and deny what was happening, very much like those dreams about death I'd often have. It was kind of an inner death, in spite of my imaginative wandering to a far off place, like a sunny, sandy, mental beach in Hawaii. Over time I was able to numb myself so that I didn't feel the physical or the emotional pain. The good part of being able to numb myself was the obvious; I didn't have to feel or think about what Jerry was doing to me. The bad part was that I couldn't control the numbness and limit it to my feelings surrounding Jerry's victimization. I lost emotion and a passion for everything in my life, including for life itself. I became so numb that nothing mattered anymore. The numbness seeped into every relationship I had. I hurt a lot of people because I couldn't feel, and for that I remain truly sorry.

My behavior fell right in line with the silence that is traditionally seen in sexual victimization of children cases. The silence surrounding victimization of all kinds, but especially sexual victimization, is dangerous to the child and advantageous to the offender. Victimization perpetrated within a relationship dynamic is one of the least talked about events in human life. Its victims are far more often silent than they are vocal.

What was more, I had been taught from a young age that my feelings and thoughts didn't matter. On top of that, Jerry was always informing me of his power and how law enforcement was waiting for me to slip up and if I didn't protect the family, I would be arrested and would rot in a jail cell. No one would believe me. My word over Jerry's word didn't stand a chance. Nobody would care what had happened to me.

Nice as it could be at times, life at Jerry's kid-friendly house was all a big façade. To keep up the façade you had to keep your mouth shut. Since circumstances kept drawing me back there, that is what I did. I came back; I stayed; and I kept my lips sealed.

CHAPTER TEN:

The Deafening Silence - Why It Is So Difficult to Tell

In her exploration of domestic violence in upscale homes, Weitzman talks about how long it took her patients to disclose the victimization to anyone. This was true in spite of the women being, in many cases, well-educated, resourceful, and having access to professional counselors. These women felt the great taboo that surrounds victimization of any kind. The fact that this is true of some of the world's most aware and affluent people should make it less difficult to imagine that it would be true of a shy, scared little boy up against the powers of the adult world. Victimization is singularly disempowering. Even grown men who for many years carried the psychological burden of having been victimized as a child, find it hard to disclose. In fact, most men in this situation fight strenuously to keep their victimization secret for the rest of their lives. I will explore some of the reasons why in this chapter.

Weitzman's patients had husbands who lavished them with fabulous homes, beautiful clothes, to-die-for vacations, opulent lifestyles, and every luxury except safety. In some ways, these things alone kept the women silent. They had social images to keep up. They had a lifestyle for themselves and for their children that they didn't want to jeopardize.

In many cases, they had a relationship that they wanted to work out. They'd built an image in their minds about how amazing it would be to be in this relationship with this wealthy man that they loved. Some had children through the marriage. Everything probably seemed great until he started abusing them. For a time, denial sets in. "This can't be happening. This wasn't how it was supposed to be. This must just be some kind of a fluke or a price I have to pay for having an otherwise great life."

Rocking the boat by disclosing victimization is difficult under any circumstances. Apparently, it has its own special difficulties when that boat is a yacht.

There were other factors in place among Weitzman's abuse patients too. Although their husbands were rich, the women themselves were not necessarily rich on an individual basis, and their husbands often controlled the purse strings, so the women were not sure they had the resources to take on the life consequences of disclosure. (Domestic offenders are usually control freaks, so it is no wonder many of them held the purse strings.) Therapists and doctors hesitated to bring up the taboo subject of domestic abuse, even when they saw the bruises (one doesn't want to offend a wealthy client, of course). Some friends and relatives thought their wonderful lifestyle should have been enough for the women; after all, their husbands were clearly good providers in spite of their faults. As mentioned above, some of the women themselves thought taking the victimization was just part of the deal (as I thought Jerry providing for me was part of an unspoken deal that I shouldn't disclose).

The victimized women also told themselves that this simply did not happen, not to people like them. Domestic abuse only happened to the poor and uneducated. They hid behind a wall of shame and denial that reinforced their silence.

This is true of victimized people of any socio-economic situation. Victimized people are often the most silent people in the world due to shame and denial. That silence can be deadly.

The "whys" of the silence are complex. In my own case, it was extremely difficult to imagine that anything good would come out of telling the truth. I was not going to mess up my life. By the time I had grown into manhood, my reasoning was that I had survived the victimization and stayed out of prison. Nobody knew the indignities I'd suffered, and my public image as a man remained untarnished. I saw no reason to mess with that. I knew Jerry could protect me from many things if I kept his secret, and I needed his protection. There seemed to be no reason to tell anyone anything, since the benefits of being Matthew Sandusky were pretty great.

People have questioned why I didn't disclose sooner what Jerry had done to me all those years. To help people understand the answer to that question, I will go into the reasons why sexually victimized children in general are hesitant to disclose. They are at least as reluctant, if not more so, to disclose than people who have suffered other kinds of victimization.

Speaking from my own experience and those of other survivors of child sexual victimization, I can say that it is never easy to admit, even to yourself, what went on behind closed doors. It's not so clear-cut to a kid or an adolescent or even an adult what really happened back then with someone who is otherwise a really nice guy. It is so personal, so private, so hidden, involving parts of the body you never let anyone see. It feels shameful. You are ashamed to admit to it. You feel guilty. You feel embarrassed. You feel dirty. As Victim Number One put it, "I felt gross and just knew I couldn't tell anyone."[7]

Survivors share a sense that no one must ever know about this. It has to be hidden in the deepest, darkest, most inaccessible part of the self. Unfortunately, this works against offenders being stopped, but it is a very real phenomenon among survivors of child sexual victimization.

Sometimes sexually victimized children are deeply attached to their offenders, as I was to Jerry. They may enjoy aspects of being intimate friends with the offender, because offenders are most often people that the kids—and their parents—know, love, and trust. Kenneth V. Lanning of the FBI wrote a report entitled, "Child Molesters: A Behavioral Analysis" for the National Center for Missing and Exploited Children. Lanning said, there are "molesters who may be their teacher, coach, clergy member, therapist, or Internet 'best friend forever' (BFF) and whose only distinguishing characteristics are they will treat the children

---

7 Aaron Fisher, *Silent No More* (New York: Ballantine Books, 2012) p. 29.

better than most adults."[8] If the offender's only real distinction (besides the victimization) is that he treats the kid better than most adults do, it is understandable why the victimized children hang onto the relationship and fear jeopardizing it by telling.

In so many ways, the cards are stacked against victims of child sex crimes disclosing. It is a kind of "conspiracy of silence" made up of emotional bonds, misplaced but very real trust in the offender, and the complicity of otherwise caring and responsible adults who also think the offender is a great guy and want the children in their care to spend more time with him. The child may be complicit too: as Lanning said, "The idea child victims could simply behave like human beings and respond to the attention and affection of offenders by voluntarily and repeatedly returning to an offender's home" is beyond many people's comprehension.[9]

Approximately, 93% of child sexual victimization is perpetrated by people the children know (and often like or love). Children sometimes don't tell due to fear of getting that person in trouble or for others reasons relating to their relationship with the person. As I have said before, child sexual victimization is not as black and white as we would like to believe it to be. It is important not to assume that if a child is not running, screaming, from the offender and telling other adults at the earliest possible opportunity, there is no victimization going on. The taboos against telling are too strong for any of us to assume that.

Child sexual victimization is one of society's best-kept secrets, even though the U.S. Centers for Disease Control and Prevention (CDC) reported in early June, 2015, in its *Morbidity and Mortality Weekly Report* that at least 25% of females and 10% of males report experiencing a form of sexual violence as a child. "Sexual violence" was defined by the CDC not only as forced assault—it ran the gamut from unwanted touching, unwanted attempted sex, pressured or coerced sex, and forced

---

8 Ibid.

9 http://www.missingkids.com/en_US/publications/NC70.pdf

sex. Girls were more likely to be victims of completed acts of unwanted sex than boys.[10] The key word here is "report." These statistics only capture what the people are willing to admit to. Like me, the majority of victims will not disclose their own victimization. Consequently, these numbers likely underreport the actual levels of victimization that has occurred.

Think of ten children you know—kids in your neighborhood, kids in school, kids who are friends with your kids, and include your own children in that count if you have them. Statistically, two or three of those familiar faces is a mask hiding an inner world of overwhelming pain and fear. Since those are only the figures on reported child sexual victimization, imagine what the real numbers are. Imagine how the numbers would skyrocket if child sexual victimization weren't something that is so relentlessly kept in the closet, often for psychological reasons the victim doesn't understand but feels powerfully, often over a lifetime. All this contributes to the deafening silence.

A victim of child sex crimes will not just "outgrow" it. It will be with them for a very long time unless someone helps them to face it, open up about it, get treatment administered by a professional trained in this particular field, embark on the road to recovery, and thus overcome it. Even then it will not be easy. But there is hope. Breaking the deafening silence about child sexual victimization is the first step toward liberation. Disclosure, difficult as it is, leads to freedom.

Of course, the offender has a keen self-interest in keeping the child silent and may use anything from bribery to threats to the child and his or her family. Sometimes all it takes to buy the child's silence is the implied threat of the withdrawal of the love, support, and gifts the offender gives. Add to that the fear and powerlessness a child feels, living in a world of giants, and you have someone who just might be silent to the grave.

In my case, Jerry, the perpetrator, had enormous perceived power in the community, in contrast to the vulnerability of the

10 http://time.com/3909006/sexual-violence-against-children-is-a-world-wide-problem-study-says/.

people he was assaulting. As one of his victims said in court, explaining why he didn't tell: "Who would believe you? He's an important guy. Everybody knows him. He was a football coach. Who would believe kids?"

It is enormously difficult to admit, even to yourself, what was done to you. For male victims of male offenders, there is the added fear that the sexual acts done to you, or which you were manipulated or forced into doing, may say something about your own sexuality. There is fear of how people will think of you, look at you or judge you—there is fear of how you will look at or judge yourself. There is shame that this happened to you, even if it wasn't your fault. All these confusing factors add to the wall of silence that surrounds child sexual victimization—and, sometimes inadvertently, help it to continue.

I mentioned earlier that when I, Jerry Sandusky's adopted son, agreed to testify against him, it was the turning point in his trial. Before that I had been an apparently ardent supporter, standing with the family behind their wall of denial that this could be happening, apparently supporting those who believed Jerry could not possibly be guilty. He had schooled me so often not to tell, not to let on, not to blow away the huge smoke and mirrors act he had going to conceal his deeds with me and many other boys. I was in as much denial as his wife, my adoptive mother, Dottie and the others were. I had never told anyone what Jerry had done to me, and I never had any intention of doing so. I knew he'd never say anything about it, so my lips were sealed, as are the lips of so many victims of the kind of sexual assaults I suffered.

"Don't tell" is the normal motto among those who endure child sexual victimization. My deep silence on the matter was par for the course, and extremely common among victims.

Some of Jerry's victims, including myself, did not disclose until the time of the trial, even though we were adults by then and knew very well that what Jerry had done to us was wrong (a child might not know this and might think it is the just way the offender relates to people). People wonder why these victims finally disclosed Jerry's crimes. I can only say that there is strength and solidarity in numbers. Once a couple of people came forward, it became easier for others to come forward too. Disclosure requires a lot of support.

Anyone who believes I made all this up to get money from Jerry, Penn State, or any other entity is dead wrong. I would never put myself, or my family through all of this pain, suffering, turmoil and public harassment for any amount of money. I am doing this, I am telling the truth, so that other boys and men don't have to suffer for decades like most of Jerry's victims have suffered. There is no way in hell that I did this for the money. I did it because Jerry Sandusky, local football hero, altruistic savior to many thousands of kids, foster father to twenty-four kids, adoptive father to six kids including me, husband to Dottie, and all-around nice guy, groomed me and sexually assaulted me and a number of other boys on numerous occasions over the course of a few decades... and he should pay for those crimes.

My previous non-disclosure does not negate the disclosures I am making now. As I am hoping to make clear, non-disclosure of child sexual victimization is the norm, not the exception.

Some do not disclose because they are afraid no one will believe them. From my own experience, I can say that there are people who will attack your credibility once you do disclose. They will claim they know more than you do about what went on behind closed doors; they will impugn your motives for saying what you said. They will re-victimize the victim by not believing him or her. They will engage in "victim-blaming," attacking the very people who were taken advantage of in the first place.

Some of this disbelief is understandable in light of the lack of knowledge on the part of the public about "nice guy" child molesters. Offenders are not necessarily "monsters" in all aspects of their lives. Some of them, like Jerry Sandusky, hold respectable positions and are contributors to society in other ways. As Lanning said, "Pedophiles span the full spectrum from saints to monsters. In spite of this fact, over and over again pedophiles are not recognized, investigated, charged, convicted, or sent to prison, simply because they are 'nice guys' . . . the media and society still view as a contradiction the fact that someone could be a caring, dedicated teacher (e.g., clergy member, coach, doctor, children's volunteer) and sexually victimize a child in his care."

These "acquaintance offenders" often get away with child sexual victimization for long periods of time—some are never exposed and caught—because they are "nice guys" and even pillars of the community. Lanning notes with great honesty that, in fact, the child sexual offenders he has talked to in the course of his work really were nice guys in every other way except for the child sex crimes that they commit. That's why CSV is so devastating—and leads to so much disbelief—when the community good guy is suddenly brought up on charges of child molestation. The offenders might be, as Lanning notes, "Big Brother of the Year, most popular teacher, or best soccer coach. It is not uncommon for these offenders to be viewed as 'child magnets' or 'pied pipers' who have an extraordinary ability to relate to children and to whom many children are drawn."

In a more recent case, J. Dennis Hastert, who served for eight years as speaker of the House of Representatives, was paying a former student hundreds of thousands of dollars to keep silent about the fact that Mr. Hastert had sexually abused him decades ago. This was reported in the *New York Times* on May 29, 2015. George Dyche of Aurora, Ill., a coach who competed against Mr. Hastert's team for years, who had worked closely with him to develop the Illinois state wrestling association said Mr. Hastert "ruled his program with a calm but firm hand. He was extremely successful and respected." And he said he was stunned by the allegations.

"Of all the people in the world, it's not the Denny Hastert I know," Mr. Dyche said. "He was a man of character, a pillar in the community." As in the case of Jerry Sandusky, the critical point here is the statement, "...it's not the Denny Hastert I know." People who are closest to nice-guy, acquaintance child sex offenders are the ones most taken in by their façade because they think they "know" the man and they do not believe that someone who is a nice guy, of high character, and a pillar of the community could possibly be the kind of "monster" who molests children.

The sad fact is that no outward personality trait rules out an inner motive to sexually victimize children. Child sex offenders look and act like everyone else to the world, and they appear as persons who genuinely want to help kids, but inside they have a very different motive for being alone with kids.

That was Jerry Sandusky to a "T". That was why there were so many shock waves of incredulity, even among his closest family members. His wife, Dottie, my adoptive mother, denies any fault on Jerry's part to this day. Did she really not know? I am skeptical, but it is possible. Jerry often took kids down to the basement, where there were all sorts of videos and other games and electronic equipment, kids' clothes, a shower, and a waterbed. One victim testified he was literally calling out for help from the basement when Jerry assaulted him, but that none of the Sandusky family members who were home responded from upstairs.

Dottie almost never came downstairs to the basement. Maybe she really didn't know and thought it was just an inviolate "man cave" or "boy cave" she should leave alone. Maybe she just couldn't believe it of her generous, loving, child-benefactor husband. Or maybe she too was part of the deafening silence that surrounds child sexual victimization, a silence it is extremely difficult to break.

THE WALL OF DENIAL LEADS TO THE DEAFENING SILENCE

Denial contributes to the deafening silence about victimization of all kinds and child sexual victimization in particular. The person disclosing the victimization may not be believed, but the accused offender may also deny that anything happened. Jerry himself adamantly maintains his innocence, although if you look at his interview with The *New York Times* or read his rambling last statement in court, the chinks in his armor are beginning to show.

In the *New York Times* interview, he is vague; his body English speaks volumes as he turns away from the interviewer. He doesn't meet her eyes, and he gives a shrugging motion and trails off into an "I don't know" stance. His denials are not the least bit believable in that interview; in fact, his shifty-eyed attitude makes him appear weird at best and guilty as sin to most. He has to be coached by his lawyer not to trail off into how appealing and attractive he finds young people and to assert, without much conviction, that that attraction is not sexual.

His interview with Bob Costas is equally unconvincing from the transcript of the questions and answers, and yet the wall of denial is still up.[11]

Bob Costas led off like this: "Mr. Sandusky, there's a 40-count indictment. The grand jury report contains specific detail. There are multiple accusers, multiple eyewitnesses to various aspects of the victimization. A reasonable person says where there's this much smoke, there must be plenty of fire. What do you say?"

Jerry says, "I say that I am innocent of those charges." Then he goes on to say that he had indeed showered with children, hugged them, and touched their legs, but without sexual intent. He uses the term "horsed around with kids." When asked point blank by Costas if he is "denying that you had any inappropriate sexual contact with any of these underage boys?" Jerry replied, "Yes, I—yes I am." When Costas brings up Mike McQueary's report as well as the janitors' reports about Sandusky's shower room activities with boys, Jerry denies that they saw what they said they saw and when asked what might be their motives to lie (two separate people who did not know one another and never met) Jerry claims their motives are only to be known by asking them. He expresses little recollection of the report by the

11 Available online at http://www.nbcphiladelphia.com/news/local/Jerry-Sandusky-Full Interview-Transcript-133872303.html Tues. Nov. 15, 2011.

mother to whom he had expressed, "I wish I were dead" and claims he never said that.

Bob Costas asks, almost rhetorically, "How could somebody think they saw something as extreme and shocking as that when it hadn't occurred, and what would possibly be their motivation to fabricate it?" and once again Jerry says he would have to ask them what their motivation is. When Costas asks, "Are you sexually attracted to young boys, to underage boys? Jerry repeats the words back to him before answering, "Am I sexually attracted to underage boys?" Pause... "Sexually attracted?" Although, given the circumstances, this would be a question that should have been expected, he is clearly thrown by it and needs time to contrive an answer. You would expect any man who was not sexually attracted to boys to immediately and unequivocally deny any sexual attraction to young boys. Instead, he hems and haws and repeats the "sexually attracted" part of the question twice. Finally, he waffles around about how much he loves and enjoys young people and eventually says no. "No. No, I—I enjoy young people. I—I love to be around them. I—I—But no, I'm not, sexually attracted to young boys." This is classic avoidance, stalling for time, and—based on what he did to me alone—an out and out lie.

Of course, by the time of this interview Jerry had to put up a wall of denial as he was going on trial. Yet it was a reflection of the inward denial that he had built up over decades of rationalizing his sexual behavior with boys. As noted, despite all of this preparation, Jerry's protestations of innocence are faint at best. Yet most offenders will, of course, deny that the allegations are true and they will often, as Jerry did in a letter to the judge, begin to take the accusers to task.

In his September 27, 2012 letter to the presiding judge at his trial, The Hon. John M. Cleland, after his conviction but before sentencing, the convicted perpetrator accused others of conspiring to bring about his situation: "There were so many people involved in the orchestration of this conviction (media, investigators, prosecutors, "the system", Penn State and the accusers).

It was well done. They won!" He noted how he relived in his cell the "inconsistent and dishonest testimonies." He attacked the accusers and their families: "I have been blamed for all their failures and shortcomings, but nobody mentioned the people who spent much more time with them than I did. Nobody mentioned the impact of the abandonment, neglect, victimization, insecurity, and conflicting messages the biological parents might have had in this." Then, with almost supreme irony, he adds, "Those who have worked with troubled lives realize a common reaction for those with low self esteem is to blame others." He went on to say, "They have been rewarded for forgetting, fabricating, and exaggerating." It was all everyone else protecting themselves, he said. This is ironic when you consider that Penn State has been forced to pay out millions in damages and has suffered great losses in prestige because of Jerry Sandusky. Surely it would have been in their interests to have Jerry acquitted! Yet here are his words of denial: "The system protected the system, the media, the prosecution, the civil attorneys, the accusers. Everybody protected themselves. Penn State, with its own system, protected their public image, their decisions, and the allegations." Again, Penn State's glacial responses to recurring allegations against Jerry Sandusky have caused the university to be accused of trying to protect *him*! "The authorities were protected," he said. "Media protected their jobs and ambitions. Prosecutors protected their jobs and egos. The system protected the prosecution. As stakes became higher, people had more to protect. Civil attorneys were protected. The accusers were protected and provided access to potential financial gain, free attorneys, accolades, psychologists, and attention."

How ironic that these are some of the very things Jerry used to groom his victims into compliance and silence. Even the jury, he said, "put up a protective shield to avoid criticism from family, friends, and the public." Who would know better how to construct and fortify a protective shield than Jerry Sandusky?

In his lengthy last statement in court, Jerry seemed to be trying to convince people that he was something of a victim in the
whole thing (which enraged a lot of onlookers at the trial). Yet he
also seemed to be trying to convey the point that he is more than
the victimization he stands convicted of; that he felt and did other
things of human significance that should be taken into account
too. That is fair enough. As mentioned, child sexual offenders are
not monsters; they do not have horns and tails; they are human
beings who have gone very badly wrong in this area of their lives,
veering into the world of crimes against vulnerable children.

They also very often use their "altruistic" work with children
as an excuse for the victimization or as some sort of mitigating
circumstance to make themselves appear less guilty for the things
they did. This is part of their denial that they'd like the judge,
jury, and general public to buy: that what they might have done
to children sexually is balanced out by the other good things they
have done for juveniles.

In revealing portions of the interview with Bob Costas
which wound up edited out, Costas touched on these very types
of points: "So it's entirely possible that you could have helped
young boy A in some way that was not objectionable, while
horribly taking advantage of young boy B, C, D and E. Isn't
that possible?"

To which Jerry replied, "Well, you might think that. I don't
know. In terms of my relationship with so many, many young
people, I would guess that there are many young people who
would come forward—many more young people who would
come forward—and say that my methods and what I had done
for them made a very positive impact on their life. And I didn't
go around seeking out every young person for sexual needs that
I've helped. There are many that I didn't have—hardly had any
contact with who I have helped in many, many ways."

It seems clear that Jerry is admitting here that though he
didn't seek "out every young person for sexual needs" he did
seek out some. That is a damning admission on his part and

should be enough to quiet those extremists who are now claiming that Jerry was railroaded and was actually innocent of all charges all along.

Justifying what they do to some children because they have helped other children (and even the children they have victimized) is part of the psyche of the child sex offender who uses benevolent activities in children's company as a sort of cover for their crimes. Denial, projection of blame, and minimization of what they do to children are classic patterns of child sexual offender behavior.

On top of his own wall of denial, the child sex offender is so caught up in his nice guy image and behavior, he has convinced himself, at least to some degree in his mind, that what he did couldn't really be sexual, couldn't really be harmful. After all, he did so much good for the kids. Jerry has stated that he helped thousands of kids through The Second Mile. He said that what he did to the children was "not sexual." He used the good things he did to put up his wall of denial.

Let there be no question about this... As one of the boys he sexually victimized long-term, I can unequivocally state that Jerry Sandusky was sexually aroused every single time he sexually assaulted me. What he did to me over and over again was deliberate, calculated, and destructive, and it caused me to nearly end my own life.

Lanning notes that the classic response of child molesters is that they "seem to have an overwhelming need to convince, primarily themselves, the behavior they engaged in is not really sex, the child doesn't understand or remember the activity and is therefore not harmed, this is an expression of love and caring, and/or they are entitled to this because of the good they do. Their need to rationalize their sexual interests and behavior often leads them to be involved in 'good works' that help troubled, needy children."[12] Attorney Marci Hamilton stated: "Pedophiles

---

12 http://www.missingkids.com/en_US/publications/NC70.pdf.

often believe they did not do anything wrong in their twisted universe—they helped their victims and loved them."[13]

Yet Jerry took denial to an extreme. After his conviction on forty-five counts of child sexual victimization, Jerry released a statement through the student-run radio station PSUComMedia. com, a part of the College of Communication at Penn State. "I'm responding to the worst loss of my life," he said from prison. "First, I looked at myself. Over and over, I asked why? Why didn't we have a fair opportunity to prepare for trial? Why have so many people suffered as a result of false allegations? What's the purpose?"

He went on to accuse his accuser: Aaron Fisher, Victim Number 1 and to paint him as part of a kind of conspiracy that was out to get him: "A young man who was dramatic, a veteran accuser and always sought attention, started everything. He was joined by a well-orchestrated effort of the media, investigators, the system, Penn State, psychologists, civil attorneys and other accusers. They won."

He then went on to attack the other "accusers and their families." He said, "Evaluate the accusers and their families. Realize they didn't come out of isolation. The accusers were products of many more people and experiences than me. Look at their confidants and their honesty. Think about how easy it was for them to turn on me given the information, attention and potential perks. I never labeled or put them down or their families. I tried and I cared, then asked for the same.

This too is part of the classic child sex offender M.O. – projecting the blame on the victim/accuser. The insidious part of this is that by picking victims who are needy, who come from broken, dysfunctional homes, who get into trouble with the law, who fall into addictions and other self-destructive behavior, the offender has a ready-made defense against any disclosures or allegations made by those victims. Isn't this also one of the reasons child victims don't immediately come forward when they are victimized? After all, who would believe them when they,

13 Kurtz, op. cit., p. 16.

troubled kids, say something bad about such a revered upstanding community hero?

"Please realize all came to the Second Mile because of issues. Some of those may remain," Jerry said. "We will continue to fight. We didn't lose to proven facts, evidence, accurate locations and times. Anything can be said. We lost to speculation and stories that were influenced by people who wanted to convict me."

In asking people to look at the accusers, Jerry failed to mention that with the exception of Victim Number 1 they all had to be sought out by authorities and convinced to testify. In fact, once Victim Number 1 came forward, investigators studied Jerry's book *Touched* to find the names of other potential victims and to track them down and ask them questions about Jerry.

Jerry does not answer the question of why on earth would the "system" collaborate with these victims to bring him down with all these alleged false allegations? Did he really think that the system had any reason to go after him and to conspire to ensnare him with their lies? For what possible purpose? Investigations and trials are expensive. Penn State and The Second Mile would be formidable forces if they lined up on the side of Jerry Sandusky.

It was noted earlier that State Attorney General Kathleen Kane thought that her predecessor, Tom Corbett, might have put off investigating Jerry in a serious way so as not to interfere with his gubernatorial campaign, so much political, economic, and social clout did Sandusky, Penn State, and The Second Mile have. Corbett has been accused of not wanting the subject of Jerry Sandusky touched until after his election. In fact, when Kathleen Kane assumed the office of attorney general, she launched an investigation as to why Jerry was credibly accused in 2008 and yet only arrested a full three years later—three years during which he continued to have access to children and to Penn State facilities and privileges (which allowed him to entice his victims into personal and private times with him). She was concerned that the delay was politically motivated, due to the power and prestige of Jerry, Penn State, and The Second Mile.

However, a report based on an investigation by H. Geoffrey Moulton Jr., a Kane appointee and a former federal prosecutor, found that there was "no direct evidence that electoral politics influenced any important decision made in the Sandusky investigation" including timing. What was more, the report found that donations from The Second Mile's board members did not affect Corbett's managing of the case. At the same time, Kane and Moulton did criticize the slowness of the investigation: "The facts show an inexcusable lack of urgency in charging and stopping a serial sexual predator," said Kane, especially in the light of the facts that Jerry went on to assault young boys even after Corbett's office had jurisdiction over the case and that an official investigation regarding Jerry was launched. Corbett's office argues that no boys were assaulted during the investigation, or at least no one they knew of.

Even this statement shows a callous disregard for victims sexually assaulted by Jerry. Why don't they know this for a fact? Apparently Corbett's office made no attempt to watch Jerry during the pendency of the investigation and ensure that he had no access to children during this time. Why not?

Some of this may have been political sparring; Corbett was a Republican and Kane a Democrat.

That is not to say that Jerry was not an important Pennsylvania personage. He was important enough for there to be such speculation about why his investigation was delayed. So how on earth could Jerry think that for some reason all these people and powers lined up against him just to persecute him?

Jerry's attorney asserted after the trial and conviction that he firmly believed he was innocent and owed no one an apology.[14] At the trial itself and in his statement on radio, Jerry stated, "In my heart I know I did not do those alleged, hideous, disgusting acts."

That sounds like many layers of denial, including perhaps the implication: "In my hearts of hearts, I didn't commit those

---

14   Ibid.

acts (even if my body did) because deep down I am really a good person."

With so much denial being typical on the part of the much more powerful, adult offender, little people who are children can be forgiven for thinking, "Who on earth is going to believe me if I tell?" or "Maybe this isn't so bad and wrong after all—Mr. So-and-So is really such a nice person. Even Mommy likes him. Maybe I am the one who is wrong to feel the way I do."

In fact, children may be silent even when the offender is caught in the act.

Without words. That seems to be one of the worst aspects of child sexual victimization. It strikes its victims silent.

Even McQueary, a full-grown man, found it hard to put into words what he had seen when he was faced with reporting it to a man he looked up to, Joe Paterno. Child sexual victimization is riddled with people's inability to put it all into words, complicated by the shame and the embarrassment and sheer disbelief they feel, sometimes questioning themselves more than they question the offender. This adds to the deafening silence that surrounds child sexual victimization.

A Taboo Subject

Of course, when it comes to sexual matters, most of us have aspects of our sexuality we would rather others did not know about. It is a subject filled with taboos. All of us have secrets we would rather others not know about, even if those secrets are simply unworthy thoughts we've had about having sex with people we know would be inappropriate. We would shudder to think that the person, or our parents, or our spouse might ever find out that we harbored such thoughts even for a fleeting moment. Sometimes we've dreamed about some movie star, but would blush to admit it in front of our children or our spouse. Maybe we had a relationship we never told anyone about; maybe we used pornography in weak moments. We really don't want to disclose these things to other people. Sex is considered one of the most private, hidden things in society. We rarely bring all of our sexual fantasies and weak moments into the light. We'd simply be too embarrassed.

Clemente often says, "Sexual behavior is very private. And criminal sexual behavior is even more private, by necessity." With this kind of dark secrecy pervading all things sexual, especially criminal sexuality, imagine how confused and conflicted a young child would be about bringing such things to light. He or she really has no comprehension of what sex is. Yet he or she knows that what the offender is doing feels odd and weird, and that it seems that this is a shameful secret that must be kept—a secret no one must ever know about. After all, the child has been taught all his or her life to keep certain parts of the body covered and under wraps and not to talk about them. Some of the sexual areas of the body are also the eliminating organs, which are often a source of shame for children during toilet training or when they have "accidents" in school at a young age. For child sex crimes victims, these "no-no" areas are precisely where the predator touches and sometimes penetrates. Taboos click into place. The child victim may feel complicit in the acts because he did not know enough or was too cowed by the adult to oppose them.

In child sexual victimization literature, there is a concept known as the "compliant victim." This term in no way implies that the victim is responsible for the crimes committed against them, it merely describes the fact that the victim goes along with the offender for a wide variety of reasons. The victim may endure the victimization in order to stay in the offender's good graces, or to continue to receive the special treatment or gifts the offender is giving to them. As I mentioned, often the child will deny that anything sexual took place out of shame or fear, even when questioned by authorities. The child is compliant not because he or she likes what is going on or consents to it (legally and morally, we know that a child is not capable of giving sexual consent; a child is always considered by law to be non-consenting.) The child is compliant because of the complexities of the grooming relationship and the fear and taboo surrounding all matters sexual, a fear and taboo that rendered even an adult like Mike McQueary inarticulate and unclear when he had to face disclosing to Joe Paterno and the Penn State administrators the acutely embarrassing and horrifying things that he had seen and heard Jerry Sandusky doing to a child in the showers.

As one male victim of Jerry Sandusky said, he was a young boy living at home with a single mother. Was he supposed to tell his *mother* what was happening to him? How embarrassing would that be? Usually the last person we want to know about anything sexual in our lives—even normal, healthy sexual things—is our mother. This is precisely why parents need to create an atmosphere in which their children feel comfortable talking to them about sex. The problem is, this will never happen until those same parents are comfortable discussing sexual matters with their children.

We all know that sex and sexuality are riddled with taboos. Most children have a very hard time accepting that their parents "did it" in order to conceive them. Some children are repelled and angered by the idea. Parents, too, are very squeamish about giving their kids "the talk" about sexuality. They find it one of the hardest topics on earth to bring up and discuss without embarrassment.

Is it any wonder that sexually victimized children have an extremely hard time disclosing what happened in this sensitive and private area of human life? It is no wonder at all.

Child sex offenders span a spectrum of behaviors, but most do not use violence with their child victims, because if they did, it might cause the victims to run to another adult to tell. The thing is, child sex offenders rarely have to use violence. As we know, they use grooming and seduction; they even use love. Lanning notes, "The nice-guy offender" is someone who "seems to love and is often loved by children." This love militates against the child disclosing the actions of the child sex offender. People will do a lot for love. If they are vulnerable enough, they will at times even put up with being victimized. This is true of people much older than children. They will put up with a lot if they feel there is a chance of being loved.

Lanning notes that "children are human beings with normal needs, wants, and desires. As human beings many children are willing to trade sex, whether or not they understand what it is, for the affection and attention of a 'nice guy.' " Like me, many of child sex crimes victims may not understand, when it starts, how wrong what the offender is doing really is. It may just seem "weird," something to be endured so that the relationship can go on. As happened with me, a child who is being systematically groomed and then sexually victimized may have absolutely no idea that the activity that raises such ambivalent feelings in him or her is actually criminal. Like me, the child may know, long before any adults in the community realize it, that the community saint is something of a weirdo when he gets you alone. Yet like me, the child may be troubled by only vague misgivings, uncertainty about right and wrong, lack of clarity about what is appropriate and inappropriate. The child likely has little knowledge of sex or normal sexual behavior due to being of a young age, naïve and innocent.

Because of the complexities involved, most child sex victims do not disclose what offenders have done to them. Every child will experience the victimization and the experience of disclosure, if they ever choose to disclose, differently. But, in fact, many of them will remain silent for the rest of their lives. Sometimes it's just too painful to let it out.

Some, in fact, will deny that it ever happened at all—like I did, for a long time. They might even vehemently defend the offender against all charges. (This appears to be the case in the recent allegations made by Wade Robeson against the estate of Michael Jackson for sexually abusing Wade when he was a boy. Robeson had previously been such an adamant supporter of Michael Jackson that he was the first witness to testify in Jackson's defense at his child sex crimes trial in 2005.) We must realize that the children in our care love and trust us. Children will quite willingly climb onto the lap of a stranger, exchange hugs and kisses, hold an adult's hand trustingly, and give their unconditional love to an adult who pays attention to them and cares for them. Children are some of the most vulnerable beings in the world, and that includes emotional vulnerability. That is one of the reasons why we love them so. Unfortunately, it can leave them especially vulnerable to sexual victimization by an adult.

IF A CHILD DISCLOSES TO YOU

Children's vulnerability is supposed to cause responsible adults to feel a strong desire to protect them. I urge all responsible adults to understand this about disclosure by a child sex victim: it is almost impossible to summon the courage to do, and when we do it, it must be respected to the utmost.

Don't encourage the deafening silence that surrounds child sexual victimization in our society (and in most societies). If a child hints at it and seems ready to disclose, please listen, and please don't freak out. By maintaining a calm, even demeanor and carefully processing what the child is saying, both verbally and non-verbally, you can help protect that child from further victimization.

We must realize the importance of disclosure. Disclosure is not only important because it gives us the reason and sometimes the means (through reporting it to the proper authorities) to protect the child. It is important because that child is taking a huge leap of faith by putting his or her trust in the person he or she discloses to. This is a child who has been victimized on all the levels child sexual victimization includes—mental, physical, emotional—even soulful. Gillam says that child sexual victimization "murders the soul" of a child. That victim, that incredibly vulnerable and hurt human being, is choosing you to confide in about the most shameful, hidden, and confusing secret he or she has ever had. Please honor that. The way an adult responds to a child's disclosure of sexual victimization will help shape the direction of that child's life.

I would like to add a note on language here, and this is important if a child discloses to you too. Do not express your moral indignation in extreme terms, such as "that monster," "that horrible wretch," or "he should be drawn and quartered for ruining your life like that." Even though I understand why Gillam says this, and I have used it to illustrate the fact that such a child is indeed hurt in his or her soul, it is also important to note that when past, present, and future child sex crimes victims read and hear statements like this one, they may believe it is now their fate to be damaged goods for the rest of their lives. As informed adults we need to be responsible for what we say and how we say it. We have no idea how many our messages will reach and how we may be unintentionally harming victims with these kinds of emotional characterizations of the results of these crimes. This type of emotional labeling of the results of child sexual victimization is not factual. Child victims can survive and thrive. They can get help and live happy and healthy lives. Once again, while I appreciate the moral indignation and the realization of how serious child sexual victimization is, we must be careful how we react so that we don't deepen the wounds already there and plant negative images in the mind of a child who is already struggling hard to come to grips with all this.

Hearing a child talking about being victimized is very difficult. We may react in a variety of ways. We may even want to minimize or deny it has happened to protect ourselves from the pain of knowing about it. It is painful and embarrassing for everyone involved, especially those charged with the care and well-being of that child. Yet we must overcome our reservations and assure the child that we believe them and that they did the right thing in disclosing. If we react negatively, with disgust, or if we don't believe them, they most likely will stop talking and might never try to disclose again. This could prevent the child from getting help. It also may allow that child and others to be continually victimized by the perpetrator.

We must remember that no matter how hard it may be for us to hear what has happened to the child, it is much more difficult for the child to disclose what happened. If a child opens up to you in this way, please be sensitive to what they are saying. A child disclosing has worked up every ounce of courage they have to tell us, sometimes believing they are taking their lives or the lives of their families in their hands. It is up to us to take that information, protect the child, and get them the help they need. Never make promises you cannot keep; never let such a disclosure go, thinking, "That child could not have been serious. I simply can't believe it of So-and-So! Why, he's a pillar of the community!"

That is what I now do for my inner child. I tell him it is safe to disclose, to admit what happened, to me. I promise to take him seriously and to understand the depth of what happened to him. I assure him that he is loved and that his life is now in the hands of a caring and responsible adult—me—and that I will always honor his disclosure and take care of him.

As I said, there is hope. One of the greatest possibilities of hope is that we as a society open ourselves to the disclosure of children, and we make a safe and trustful atmosphere where they can come to tell their sorrowful, scary tales and get the protection they need and deserve.

I close this lengthy but important chapter with a quote from Brené Brown, Ph.D., LMSW. Brown is a research professor at the University of Houston, with her subjects of study being vulnerability, courage, feelings of worthiness, and shame. She has authored three *New York Times* bestsellers: *Daring Greatly: How the Courage to Be Vulnerable Transforms the Way We Live, Love, Parent, and Lead* (2012), *the Gifts of Imperfection* (2010), and *I Thought It Was Just Me* (2007).

"Owning our story can be difficult, but not nearly as difficult as spending our lives running from it. Embracing our vulnerabilities is risky but not nearly as dangerous as giving up on love and belonging and joy—the experiences that make us the most vulnerable. Only when we are brave enough to explore the darkness will we discover the infinite power of our light."

CHAPTER ELEVEN:

The Grand Jury and the Man in the Mirror

I didn't disclose Jerry's victimization to anyone as a child, and I did not intend to as an adult either. As I said, I had survived being victimized by Jerry, and he had stopped; I had avoided incarceration, finished probation, and I was now an adult. I thought I had weathered the storms and that it was time to start living as a free man.

Then something super disruptive and frightening happened. The pressure to disclose began to build because authorities wanted to talk to me about Jerry.

THE INVESTIGATION BEGINS

During the time I was back living in Jerry's home, my biological brother was under investigation for murder. The police asked me to come to the station for questioning.

I think any human being would be nervous if they were asked to come in for questioning on a murder investigation. Police procedure may be unknown to you, you do not know clearly if you are under arrest or not, you wonder if they have reason to hold you there, and you feel fearful of being trapped into saying something you shouldn't. You don't quite know what your rights are or aren't in this situation. You are unlikely to have a defense attorney's phone number programmed into your cell phone. It's not like this is a "normal" set of circumstances.

I was armpits-dripping-with-cold-sweat nervous. I was wondering if my lips were going to tremble visibly when I talked and whether their sharp eyes were going to catch every tremor. I feared I would appear guilty or as if I were hiding something whether I was or not, just because my palms were wet and my throat was dry and I could barely meet anyone's eye, I was so scared.

I was beyond nervous. I hated the police. They had not been my friends, and I was no friend of theirs either. I distrusted them hugely. I feared they might set a verbal snare for me that I would fall into. I didn't want to say anything that might incriminate my brother or get myself in trouble somehow. They certainly knew my record. I doubted if they trusted me or my word either. I could barely breathe, and my chest was tight with fear and resentment at being called down to speak to them like this.

I was locked in with them in a small, nondescript room, which made me feel trapped. I wanted to get out of there so badly. I'm sure now I was being recorded and perhaps even being watched through the one-way mirror. What was more, I sensed from the demeanor of the two Pennsylvania state troopers, one female and one male, who were there to interrogate me that there was a lot on the line. My anxiety shot up to sky-high levels. I could feel my heart pounding against my chest and my breathing was labored. I had done nothing wrong, but because of years of having to walk a fine line to avoid incarceration, I was far from at ease. I fully expected to be arrested for something at any moment while I was there.

They questioned me for about fifteen minutes, directing seemingly pointless questions at me about my brother, questions that they must have known I couldn't answer. It was disconcerting. Then suddenly they switched over to what appeared to be the real reason they had asked me to meet with them.

The female officer left the room. The male trooper was someone I knew from my time in the juvenile detention center. He had been a guard while I was being detained there. He must have thought we had some kind of a bond from that, as he spoke to me as if I could trust him and as if he wanted me to feel free to confide in him.

He then started to ask questions about Jerry. He told me that Jerry was being investigated for sexually abusing boys. He wanted to know if I believed it and if Jerry had ever done any-thing to me.

My panic had been bad enough to start with, but when he started to ask these questions, I felt as though I was going to pass out. I felt like I had been punched in the stomach. This police officer had just put me in a life-changing position, between the proverbial rock and a hard place. Now I had to choose between lying to a law enforcement officer while maintaining the sealed lips I had held for so very long and breaking the protective si-lence that I had sworn to myself I never would.

This was also the first time anyone had ever even hinted that Jerry was anything but a pillar of the community, the saint of Happy Valley. I was shocked that they were on to him like this.

Cautiously, I told the officer that I didn't believe Jerry would do any of the things the boys were accusing him of and that nothing had ever happened to me. I lied. So the officer pressed me further. I'm sure he had a strong feeling that I was not telling the truth, but I would not be deterred from my story that, as far as I was concerned, Jerry was innocent. My answer was an ada-mant no, nothing had ever happened to me at Jerry's hands, nor could I imagine it happening to other guys.

As justification for my untruthfulness on that occasion, I can only say that while I feared the police, there was one person and one thing I feared more. I could never let anyone know what Jerry had done to me. The shame and embarrassment forced me to keep my mouth shut.

When I left the police station, I went immediately to Jerry and told him what the police had asked me about him and what they had told me. The only thing on my mind was that I didn't want Jerry thinking I had said anything to them. I didn't want him thinking that I had exposed what he had done to me for so many years.

To my mind, the police had thrown my life into chaos by asking me the questions they had asked. If Jerry didn't believe that I had remained silent, he would report me, and he would see to it that I went to prison. I was certain of that. I didn't know at the time that Jerry's power and influence were already on the wane. He no longer had the reach of a god in Happy Valley. He was under investigation for multiple counts of child sexual victimization.

As it turned out he believed me that I hadn't said anything to the police. Then he and Dottie had a conversation about needing to tell the other kids in their home that Jerry was being investigated for these kinds of activities.

In fact, from that moment, Jerry started to groom the family once again, only in a different way; he needed to groom them to say the right things so that he would not be arrested for child sexual victimization. It was time to make sure we all understood that it was us against the world, and that we all had to stick together.

I am left thinking why would Dottie feel the need to tell the other kids if she did actually believe Jerry was innocent? If he was innocent, then the other kids would naturally defend him. Anything they said would help his case. They wouldn't need to prep the kids to say the right things in that case. Why hadn't they told us that he was under investigation if they already knew? I suppose it was because Jerry was such an expert groomer. Now he needed his skills again.

PRESSURE COOKER

The police would not let up their pressure on me. They must have been pretty certain that Jerry had victimized me. Apparently they thought that putting me before a grand jury would make me change my mind and tell the truth, so I was summoned to appear. When he found out about my summons, Jerry scheduled a meeting with an attorney who had worked with many grand juries. Jerry and I went to see the attorney together.

The lawyer went over what it would be like and what to expect. Jerry and I had many talks about the exact words I should use so that there would be no question about what I was saying. I would go over to his house, he would call me upstairs to his office, and we would practice. He would tell me he loved me and that the family had always been here for me and now it was my turn to return the favor. In retrospect these actions on Jerry's part may amount to the crime of obstruction of justice, and suborning perjury. He wasn't simply encouraging me to remain silent before the grand jury, he wanted me to lie to them.

I drove to Harrisburg, Pennsylvania with my future wife Kim the night before my grand jury testimony. We were put up in a hotel. While we were there my anxiety became so intense, I told Kim I needed to go for a walk. I ended up walking by the river. There was a concrete walkway that ran right along the water.

For the second time in my life I contemplated suicide. I would stand there on one foot while I held the other over the water, balancing and wondering whether I should just let go. The water level was high and the river was moving swiftly. I figured I would be taken under and would drown quickly.

I couldn't bring myself to do it, though. I collapsed on the ground until an intense panic attack passed and the adrenaline stopped pumping through me. When my heart rate slowed down and I was breathing normally, I then walked back to my hotel and decided to prepare myself as well as I could for the next day.

There was the truth, waiting to be told. There was Jerry's awesome power in the community and this, the beginning of his downfall. I considered all I owed him and all I despised about him. I felt the intensity of my gratitude and my resentment, my complicity and my resistance. Pure ambivalence. There was my love and my hate. He had been like a father to me and had opened up whole new worlds of opportunity and joy to me—yet mingled with the kindness was the fact that he had taken advantage of that to molest me. On top of that, there were my fear and mistrust of the police, my worries about my own record with them, and Jerry's involvement in keeping me out of jail. There was my dislike and fear of buildings like jails and courthouses and people having to do with the law. I also knew that I had been coached by a pro to commit perjury and commit it credibly. I knew that perjury was a serious crime and, if discovered, could land me in prison. At the same time, the idea of publicly acknowledging that Jerry had done those things to me seemed incredibly humiliating and shaming to the point of being impossible to do.

Believe me, with all those conflicting pressures working on me, I wanted to find some way out. Yet I knew the bottom of the river wasn't it. But I also knew that if Jerry was out of the equation, if his influence and grooming and coaching my testimony didn't happen, I would have succumbed to the pressure of telling the truth about him.   Unfortunately, at the time and with Jerry's influence so real and overwhelming, I kept my silence about the crimes he committed against me. I protected Jerry and the family name. I lied for him as much as I lied for me.

Default Mode

The next morning I went to the building where the grand jury proceedings were being held. I was placed in a room with the same therapist from The Second Mile I had met with so many years ago. He was very kind and courteous to me, treating me almost as if we were friends. If he only knew the damage that his betrayal had caused me at a young age and until this point in my life, surely he would understand we were not friends, nor would we ever be. He was the one who, when I confided to him in therapy, went and told Jerry everything I said, shutting the door to disclosure to a mental health professional for a long time to come. How was I supposed to disclose my secret shame and suffering now, when for all I knew, that person would go right to Jerry and tell him all I said?

I had been sent to The Second Mile because of mistrust of grown men in the first place. Then Jerry had his way with me. Everyone in the community supported and applauded Jerry and thought he was the best thing that ever happened to kids like me. That meant that trusting representatives of the community, law enforcement, and the therapeutic community wasn't really an option for me. My faith in them was completely ruptured.

When I was called to testify, I walked into a large conference room that was filled with what seemed like fifty people. I was at the front of the room, and I had the assistant DA and the same male state trooper I had talked to down at the police station asking me questions.

I think it is understandable that I went into default mode. I'd been schooled by Jerry for years never to tell, never to disclose. I had denied what was happening all along, sometimes even to myself. Before the grand jury, I did what I had always done and what Jerry and I felt his lawyer had wanted me to do: I denied everything and said I couldn't believe that any of the allegations against Jerry were true. I said it all just the way Jerry had prepared me to say it.

I'm sure many people wonder why I didn't take the opportunity, under oath in a court of law, to tell the truth about Jerry at that time. I can only explain that along with my fear of Jerry and his social and financial power, the shame and guilt over what Jerry had done to me would not allow me to tell the truth. I was afraid of being outed to the world as a man that had been forced to have obscene sexual acts performed on me by another man, and that he had forced me to do the same to him. The stigma of that is pretty intense. Men have a lot of pride about their masculinity. To admit that something like that was done to you means to admit that you are broken, that you were overpowered, that another male dominated you shamefully. It doesn't help that much to realize that you were a kid, practically helpless, up against a male twice your size and full of wiles and deceits that confused your young mind.

Part of the problem is that because you have matured, you look back on what was done to you and what you were forced to do with the eyes of an adult. It is impossible for you to recreate the naiveté that you possessed at the time you lost your innocence. So, you almost can't help but judge your child-self in a more harsh and damning manner. This only adds to your desire to keep all of this secret. You feel like you are damaged goods.

Admitting and showing that damage to the world in some way makes you feel responsible and to blame. The way people look at you after that—believe me, it takes more courage than I had at that time. I believe I was more afraid of public disclosure than I was of going to prison for perjury.

After I finished my testimony, I went back downstairs and met up with Kim. While upstairs she had gone to the gift shop and purchased a little card that had a nice love poem and the words "I love you" across the top. It was what I needed more than anything in that moment. I still carry that card in my wallet to this day, and any time I get down or start feeling unworthy of love, I take it out and read it. It's my daily reminder that I am valuable and deserving of being loved unconditionally.

Jerry's Defender?

We left Harrisburg right away and headed straight to Jerry's house. I once again made him understand that I had said nothing had happened between us and that I had expressed disbelief about the things others were saying about him.

While I was at his house, I had an interesting experience. I received two phone calls, both from people who were very close to Jerry. I had not spoken to either of them very much in the past. Now they both told me how proud of me they were and how I had done the right thing. I was disgusted and wanted to throw up. It was the first time that I thought maybe there were more people out there who were like Jerry. I couldn't think of any other explanation as to why these two almost complete strangers would call me and congratulate me on what I knew was a lie.

Over the next few months to a year (I'm not really clear on the time span) I was trying to distance myself from Jerry. He was going to go on trial for molesting other boys, but I just wanted to live my own life. I had met a great woman who finally had shown me what unconditional love is, and we were planning on getting married. Kim and I were married in December of 2011 and planned to go forward in life with raising children. To this day my wife and my children show me what a gift life truly is every day. They are all blessings and a huge part of my healing journey.

All I wanted to do at this point of my life was to enjoy being a man with a good and growing relationship with his wife and family. I would have liked to have forgotten that Jerry had ever been a part of my life. But Jerry was hell bent on having me once again testify in his favor. He wanted me to take the stand at his trial and once again lie.

I didn't want to lie in court. I'd done it once in the grand jury; it was over. I hadn't got caught, but I wanted out. Why couldn't it all just go away? I wasn't going to tell the truth to the world, but I didn't want to perjure myself again either. Why did Jerry have to keep pressuring me? Why couldn't he leave me alone?

People have claimed that I supported Jerry up to this time, and they see that as an indication that I am lying about being victimized by him. However, this is far from the truth. I never supported Jerry. I lied because of the pressures I have described. I lied for my own self-preservation and the pressures he brought to bear on me. It had nothing to do with anything else. Also, in spite of the accusations against him, I did not know whether he had victimized others or not. Like many child sex crimes victims, I always thought I was the only one. This thinking didn't change overnight. I was not about to be the one who stood alone and accused Jerry in open court. I had no idea what the consequences of doing that would be. This had all become way too big for me to handle.

The evening before the trial, I made the very difficult decision to go and ask Jerry not to call me as a witness. He had upped his persuasions to get me to testify for him, and I did not want to take part. I knew I had to plead with him not to call me.

I went to his home and asked Dottie to leave the room. It was a hard conversation, but I asked him not to call me as a witness because I remembered things that had happened between us. His response was that those things were "not sexual." This is the only time he has ever spoken about what he did to me, actually admitting that he had in fact done "things" to me. Yet he was deeply entrenched in so much denial. Even after all the accusations came out during trial and he was convicted on 45 counts of child sexual victimization, he denied that anything he had done with children was sexual. He always characterized it as just "horsing around." That kind of denial is not unusual in child sex offenders, but I didn't know that at the time, so I didn't elaborate; I didn't go into more details about the past; I just asked him not to call me as a witness. He eventually agreed but he had a stipulation. He wanted me to drive Dottie home from court the next morning. He said he didn't want her to have to drive the ten miles home from court by herself. I agreed. It seemed an innocent enough request and not too much to ask, especially since he was letting me off the hook of testifying and committing perjury again.

I still wasn't able to see the manipulation and control he had over me. I am certain he knew that if I left that courtroom when Dottie did, in her presence, driving her home, I would be seen as a supporter. It was a public relations coup for him, all right. People already knew I had testified on his behalf in front of a grand jury. When I was seen leaving with other witnesses in his favor, and driving his wife (who still staunchly denies that Jerry ever did anything criminal), that would seal my fate. I would be seen as being on his side: the adopted child Jerry had so generously raised as his own, who knew Jerry personally and up close and who stood by his side against all the awful allegations.

With this one brilliant defensive maneuver he accomplished several things. Of course, he could still call me as a witness, but now there wasn't even any need. I had stood with him publicly even though I didn't want to. What was more, if I ever came forward to tell the truth, my credibility would be undermined since in his highly publicized trial, I appeared to be among the witnesses who supported him. This was his mastermind brilliance at play; remember his strategic thinking was way above average, as testified to by the exceptional defensive strategies he'd developed for Penn State's Nittany Lions.

Driving back to the town of State College, I wondered if Jerry would really make good on his word not to call me as a witness. I wondered if he felt he had already gotten all he could out of me by manipulating me to be seen taking care of his wife.

I felt I had to stand up for myself and protect myself against his machinations. I had to take my life back from his control. I knew that I needed to sit in open court and stop him from calling me as a witness or all this would drive me crazy. So I went back to court as his trial continued to make sure I stayed off the witness list.

Little did I know how that simple act, that decision to stand up for myself, would forever change my life.

Epiphany

While sitting there in court I heard the testimony of one of Jerry's victims. They called him Victim Number 4. As he spoke, so courageously, so honestly, I realized that he was telling my story too. Every detail he stated about what Jerry had done to him, Jerry had done to me as well. It was because child sex offenders follow a pattern they carefully develop over their offending careers, but I didn't know that at the time. All I knew was that it was as if Victim Number 4 was holding up a mirror to my life and making me look into it clearly for the first time. It was so surreal, I wondered how he could possibly know what had happened to me in such detail. His story was virtually the same as mine.

It was the first time that I knew for certain that I was not Jerry's only victim. Until that very moment, I believed I was the only one. I had witnessed many things with Jerry and other children, yet when I saw other boys being soaped up or touched in certain ways, because my self-image was so broken, I never related it to Jerry sexually victimizing other boys; I always saw it as a primer for me. My young brain could not comprehend the idea that he was doing this to others. I could only see myself as weak. Nobody else would allow this to happen. That was the way I thought, that I was completely broken.

For me, I am lucky that the courage and honesty of Victim Number 4 unfolded right in front of me in the courtroom. I couldn't run away from that. All the illusions about Jerry were stripped away. "Pay no attention to that man behind the curtain!" could no longer keep up the facade. I heard my own story in Victim Number 4's, down to a "T". I recognized the patterns of behavior; I understood that this guy, Victim Number 4, had filled a spot I once did—one of the kids Jerry moved on to after I "aged out" of his preferred age span and began to act in such a way as to tell the world with my deeds what I could not say with my words—that I was being intolerably victimized. I realized in that moment that when my victimization ended, Victim Number 4's soon began along with a few other boys between our victimizations.

As the man on the stand told his story, I saw how Jerry had "groomed" him with increasingly inappropriate touching, friendliness, intimacy, care, and help—just like he had groomed me. He took him to games, to the athletic facilities, and gave him privileges that only the great Jerry Sandusky could bestow. The grooming was a mirror image of my experiences.

It became impossible to deny. The baton of Jerry's sexual victimization had been passed from me to Victim Number 4. He was not the next direct victim after me but he was soon after. Victim Number 4 wasn't running with it. He was handing it over to the judge and the jury.

His courage blew me out of the water. Here was someone who was facing a courtroom with the offender in it, looking right at him, defying an inflamed public, and bringing all the hidden, shameful, embarrassing things right out in the open, right into the light of day where everyone could see them.

The courage it takes to disclose should never be discounted. This is true even when a person discloses privately let alone publicly. I am grateful to every survivor of child sexual victimization who discloses, because it opens the dark closet and lets the sunlight in, shining the truth on that which festers, unchecked, in the darkness.

As I contemplated the incredible bravery and truthfulness of Victim Number 4, I knew I had the choice whether I was going to continue living a lie or begin to be as valorous, open, and honest as that person.

I chose the latter. I realized I could stay silent no longer.

That's the "why" of my willingness to testify and that's the "why" of my work ever since: my work with the Peaceful Hearts Foundation, and the "why" of this book. There is no other reason. There was no other reward. The greatest reward has been the healing that has come into my life because I opened a hideous sore, let the pus run out in the most public of settings, and let the sunshine dry up the infection and heal the wound.

It wasn't easy, as anyone knows who has disclosed something of consequence in a public forum. The first step is definitely the hardest; to admit to other people (and finally to yourself) the nature of your difficulties. Letting others know is the hardest part. This is why, I believe, Alcoholics Anonymous has everyone who wants to speak out at a meeting introduce themselves by saying, "I am an alcoholic." Every time someone admits that about themselves, to others in a public forum, more of the pus runs out, more of the disease is exposed to the fresh air and sunshine. Disclosing is the first step toward healing.

Victim Number 4's testimony hit me like the proverbial ton of bricks. Jerry had me convinced that these men accusing him were only out for money, but as I listened to Victim Number 4, I realized that couldn't be true. He knew too much; he had endured the same indignities that I had, letter for letter, point by point. This all too familiar story made me realize that the other accusations against Jerry were true, and that I was but one in a long line of victims.

Victim Number 4 also acknowledged that he had denied what had happened to him for a very long time. He acknowledged that he had lied to the police and even to his own lawyer about the victimization. All I could do was bow my head and shake it from side to side. How alike we were.

I marveled at the courage this man showed. He not only sat in front of his victimizer and told the truth about him, he told the world about it too. He sat in front of complete strangers and revealed this most intimate of violations, with all its implications and repercussions, in open court.

Shaken, I realized I was now faced with a crucial decision as to what to do. Would I spend the rest of my life protecting a child sex offender with my silence, or would I be able to show the fortitude of Victim Number 4 and tell the world what Jerry had done to me? Should I, at long last, open the closet full of secrets and power plays meant to keep me silent and the ever-present violation of my personhood? Should I let the light of truth shine into that basement of hidden, dark things? Should I let myself out of that suffocating space after having kept it hidden for so long? Should I acknowledge that Jerry wasn't keeping me safe; he was keeping me imprisoned in the jail of my own silence?

I spent the next day or so in a haze. I would just lie on the couch or go for long walks with no real destination in mind. I couldn't rationalize what was happening, and I didn't know how to handle it. I had never spoken out loud the words about what Jerry did to me, year after year. Nor did I think that I ever would. I wore my silence like an iron shield. Yet here I was, contemplating going to the police, the people I had always feared, the people Jerry had always protected me from to finally tell the truth.

Did I shed tears? Yes. Was I frightened? Yes. Was it the biggest decision I had ever made in my life? Absolutely.

I went into my bathroom and looked myself in the eyes in the mirror and said out loud, "What are you going to do? Are you going to remain the coward you have been and not say anything, or are you going to make the difficult choice to tell the truth, and risk losing everything?"

The next words out of my mouth would forever change the course of my life.

My own reflection said to me, "You were sexually victimized by Jerry Sandusky and you no longer have to be afraid. It is time to take a stand for you."

CHAPTER TWELVE:

The Power and Perils of Disclosure

After reaching my decision I knew that I had to tell my wife. I had to tell Kim that I too was a victim of Jerry's, and to alert her and consult with her as to what my next steps were going to be. I picked up the phone and dialed her work number. I told her I needed to speak with her as soon as possible, and that it was important. She managed to get off work and came right home. She had been able to tell that this was a crucial moment for me, and that I had a deep need of her support and counsel without delay.

We sat down and had one of the hardest conversations I've ever had to have. I have mentioned in a previous chapter what kind of issues hold people back in general from disclosing child sexual victimization, and I've also gone into why I in particular held back from telling anyone about me being victimized at Jerry's hands. Disclosing to my wife was a revolutionary step for me. For the first time I was finally able to verbalize to another person that I was sexually victimized as a child. You can't help but wonder what people will think, even your own loving wife. It isn't a nice thing to have to admit to. It was a pretty ugly truth, and I had never dreamed of telling anyone on earth about it before.

Kim was completely supportive and loving. She was so understanding. She didn't judge me; she wasn't repelled; and her belief in me was total. Kim gave me the emotional support I so desperately needed. We hugged and she reassured me that she would always be by my side, and we would get through all of it together. The relief was overwhelming.

If you've ever carried a festering secret that long and then finally exposed it to the light of truth, you can understand the incredibly liberating feeling I had after I finally told someone who not only believed me but understood. I felt like my mind had been a swollen wound full of infection and pus, and I had lanced it and all the poisonous junk had flowed out. The sense of release was incredible; it brought us so close that it seemed like, after that, we would be able to bear any consequences of the disclosure together.

It was important to me that Kim believed me. When you finally choose to disclose something so deep, so personal, so buried, it is especially important when people give credence to what you have said.

For example, Victim Number 1 bonded with the psychologist of Children and Youth Services, Michael Gillum, right away because Gillum believed him. Aaron was just fifteen at the time he disclosed about Jerry to officials of his high school in Pennsylvania. Even the authorities at his own school were incredulous at first, because they kept saying Jerry Sandusky had a heart of gold and was one of the pillars of the community. In fact, instead of making an immediate phone call to the police or CYS, as was required of them in their positions as educators making them mandated reporters, they advised Victim Number 1's mother and him to think about it overnight. They just couldn't believe it of Jerry, who frequently came to the school to pull Victim Number 1 (Aaron Fisher) out of classes to "mentor" him and who volunteered as a coach for the high school football team. In their minds it just couldn't be true of "nice guy" Jerry Sandusky who did so much for needy youth! However, their disbelief hurt Aaron and upset his mother. It's important to know that when people don't believe disclosures about child sexual victimization they are, in a sense, re-victimizing the victim by hurting him or her again. They also, however they might not mean to, collude with the silence that allows the offender to go on molesting. Fortunately, Aaron's mother did not give up and eventually these school officials believed Aaron enough to go to bat for him and notify Children and Youth Services. It was the belief of the psychologist at CYS that helped him get through the incredible ordeal he was to face in being the first victim to attempt to bring Jerry to justice. Slowly, over time, state troopers, people in the attorney general's office, and others began to believe Aaron as more and more suspicious things about Jerry surfaced. At last enough people believed him to result in Jerry's arrest.

Others' belief in the disclosure of a victim is absolutely key. It is key to the victim getting the relief and protection he or she needs, and it is also key to stopping the offender from moving on to other children. . At the very least, if a victim discloses to you, you should err on the side of caution and protect that child, report it to the police and/or Child Services and prevent the accused adult from having continued access to that child until the allegations are completely vetted.

DISCLOSURE REVEALS THE CHINKS IN JERRY'S ARMOR

There was a wall of disbelief surrounding Jerry's actions, but little by little that wall began to crumble as victims made their disclosures. It turned out that way back in 1998, a mother had contacted campus police about Jerry's inappropriate behavior with her son. Then, in 2000, a janitor told some co-workers about seeing Sandusky orally assaulting a child in the shower at Penn State. In 2001, McQueary came forward and reported to "Joe Paterno" and Penn State administrators that the former assistant coach was naked with a child in the shower and "it was way over the line" at the university's football facility. Then Victim Number 1, his mother, and CYS came forward in 2008.

Even with all these reports, it was not until 2011 that authorities felt there was enough evidence accumulated that the state could risk arresting Jerry. They had to make sure their case was airtight against such a powerful and beloved man.

Formidable powers were all lined up, it seemed, on the side of keeping Jerry behind a wall of silence and denial. All they had on the other side were a couple of extremely scared, severely traumatized kids who didn't want to tell anyone—even their own mothers—what had been done to them. I want to take this moment to discuss the importance of parents being able to help protect their children from this type of fear of disclosing. One thing that can be done is to have age appropriate conversations with your children throughout their lives so that they will feel empowered to talk to you if they have or are about to become victims of sex crimes. The conversation should start early in their lives and continue throughout into adulthood. As parents you have the responsibility to empower your children. When they witness you being able to have a hard conversation they will be more likely to come to you when they have been victimized or may be victimized.

Yet eventually the power of disclosure began to gain enough momentum to take Jerry down. People believed the victims. Their voices were at long last heard and heeded. Ultimately, that is the power of disclosure, even from a kid so scared he can barely speak, as Aaron Fisher was when authorities questioned him in court for the first time. They had to arrange it so that he would only have to answer "Yes" or "No" to questions. That's how hard it can be to disclose.

It is some testimony to the difficulty of disclosure when you realize that only one out of ten accusers spoke up to authorities about Jerry's sexual victimization on his own. The others had to be found and questioned repeatedly by authorities before they would tell their stories. They did not come forward, and their initial responses to investigators tended to be like mine: denial, denial, denial. The only one in the ring at first was Aaron Fisher, and even he would only speak to a male psychologist trained in dealing with child sexual victimization. He refused to talk to any females about it at all.

The shame and ugliness of child sexual victimization is so great, most victims never disclose. What's more, when they do, they are often not believed. This is one of the perils of disclosure. I have gone into the reasons so many victims never disclose in more detail in Chapter Eight. For now, I will only say that when people believe you and support you in your disclosure, it helps greatly on the personal level, and it is the beginning of breaking through the wall of denial that shields child sexual offenders on a public level from prosecution for their crimes. It also prevents the victims of child sex crimes from being re-victimized by people who attack them and call them liars when they have finally found to courage to bring forth their most closely held secrets.

Trust Breached

While having lunch with my wife, at a local pizza shop, on the second day of the trial I received a phone call from one of my adopted brothers. I had not reached out to him but here he was calling me, I was confused. His reason for calling, as he stated, was to encourage me that if anything had ever been done to me by Jerry that I should go to the police and disclose. In that conversation he disclosed to me that as a teenager he was victimized by Jerry, not to the level that the other victims had been but things had happened and that he knew I was victimized as well. He told me that he supported my decision to disclose if I decided to do so. I said thank you and ended the call. This conversation had a huge impact on my decision to disclose my own abuse.

After that great experience with my wife, who believed me and assured me of her love, and the phone call from my adopted brother I knew there was one other person whom I trusted enough to disclose to before I talked to the police. I called one of my Sandusky siblings with whom I had always had a strong bond. I had always been able to confide in this person during difficult times. Upon setting up arrangements, my wife and I drove to the Sandusky home and picked this person up. We drove back to Kim's and my home where we could have some privacy, and I sat on the couch with this person. I disclosed to this trusted person that our adoptive father had sexually victimized me.

This person looked me in the eyes and expressed belief in me. The person had even also had an epiphany in court that day, saying, "The name of my book came to me today; it will be entitled *My Dad Is a Pedophile*." I was so relieved that the person had faith in me, accepted me, and believed me. We hugged, and Kim and I thanked the person for listening and for being supportive. Disclosing is so much easier when people support you, especially those who matter to you.

Unfortunately, the person's belief in what I disclosed was not genuine, or it simply did not last. In fact, my disclosure would signal the last conversation I would ever have with that person or any Sandusky family member. My former adoptive siblings turned on me and would later use my trust as a way to try to paint me as a villain. This hurt me tremendously.

I had enough faith in these people to disclose the awful things that had happened to me for so many years, things I had kept hidden deep within me. I brought the dark, awful secrets out into the light of day, trusting these people enough to share the most sordid things. After listening to me bare my guts and open the deepest locked doors of my heart, these people would then shun me and publicly come forward and characterize my disclosure as an attempt at "trying to turn the family to my side" against Jerry. The brother who had called me, reached out to me, would call again. This time he informed me that if I ever spoke about what he told me that his high powered attorney would sue me for everything I had.

I felt totally betrayed. There were no sides to take in this. This wasn't "us against them," our family against the world, or something some side could win and the other side would lose. Child sexual victimization is not a game. There are no winners and losers. As the mother of Victim Number 6 said after Jerry's conviction, "Nobody wins. We've all lost." Nor is it a prize to be labeled publicly as a child sex crimes survivor; in fact, it brings problems of its own. My family has gone through hell because of my disclosure, there are times when I regret having not kept my silence. It would have been easier for all of us if I had. I certainly didn't perceive it as trying to win people over to my side. For once in my life, truth was the side I was on now. It seemed to me that was the only side anyone should be interested in.

What these people did to me was unforgivable. A person who discloses is showing deep scars and wounds to the trusted confidant. Dismissing them or disbelieving them is like rubbing salt on those deep lacerations to the psyche. I had given these people the most sacred thing I had—my trust, which had been violated so many times. I had made myself totally vulnerable through my disclosure, and they used it as a weapon to stab me in the back. They must now live with that knowledge. I suppose having something like that on your conscience is in and of itself a pretty stiff punishment. I will never give up hope that they both will find the courage to come forward and tell their truths. Overcome the fear of the Sandusky family and be free.

My mind was still in a fog after these disclosures, but emotionally I was feeling stronger because I had my wife by my side, and at the time, I thought that I had two trusted family members standing with me also. I knew there would be a risk of being accused of perjury from my former statements defending Jerry in court, so I decided to call a lawyer, rather than go directly to the police, to find out what I could do to protect myself legally.

By this time there was a wealth of evidence against Jerry, and there were 48 counts of child sexual victimization against him with multiple victims. Still, it was not easy for me to disclose to anyone else. After I called an attorney, a meeting was set up at a park and as we all sat around a brown, moss-covered picnic table, I recounted for the lawyers the truth about the sexual victimization I had suffered at the hands of my adopted father for many years.

Within the hour they facilitated a meeting at the attorney general's office. When we arrived at the office, I found out that my attorneys would not be able to be in the room, though, and I was not happy about that. As I entered a small, ten by eight room by myself, my anxiety went through the roof. My legs started to get real wobbly and my mouth instantly went dry. Sitting around the table were five grown men and myself. The idea of having to tell these men what had happened to me was not something I was prepared to do.

The shame of being sexually victimized by a man and having been silent for so long rendered me incapable of telling five complete strangers the depth of the victimization that I had suffered. The only things I could tell them at the time were the more basic types of sexual victimization I had suffered at the hands of the perpetrator they were prosecuting. I spoke in fairly general terms. It was important to me that they understand that I had lied previously and now I wanted to clear that up and come forward to speak the truth. I tried to get the point across to them that I was a victim without actually having to say the specific words outlining the sexual victimization out loud to them. I was new at this disclosure business, and I found myself only willing to draw the outlines of the victimization rather than to give them the full picture in sordid detail. I would later learn that this is extremely common with child sex victims. It is called incremental disclosure.

It seemed to be enough, though. My conversation was recorded, and I was told that a copy would have to be given to Jerry's defense team.

After I left that meeting I felt good about being able to speak the truth at last. Yet I sensed a major firestorm was coming. I had no idea just how right I was.

THE MEDIA FIRESTORM

The storm was huge, because I bore Sandusky's name, and because I was his adopted son, and because I had formerly denied the victimization. I hope by now the reader understands that denial is so much a part of being a child sex crimes victim that it is the norm, not the exception. My non-disclosure, even my denial when questioned, was usual for victims, not out of the ordinary at all. At the same time, my telling my story and finally telling the truth about what I had experienced growing up with Jerry was a bombshell in the case. The media was going to have a field day with that. What was more, one of the attorneys called me later that evening and informed me that somehow the media had received a copy of my confidential disclosure and that on the morning news they would be playing parts of it for the world to hear. This was a devastating violation of trust.

My world started to crumble. I felt like a sand castle on the beach being wiped away by the incoming tide. Everything I had built was falling apart, and I had nobody to blame but myself for disclosing. I knew I would not be the only one to suffer: my wife and children would suffer with me now. I was responsible for what was about to happen to all of them, and I will always carry that burden. We were to become the subject of all kinds of print and electronic media coverage, my name and picture plastered all over everyone's television set because of the sensational nature of the case.

It has bothered me tremendously what my family had to go through because of my disclosure. This is certainly one of the perils of disclosure, besides others' disbelief. It is the fact that the media also involves your family. Of course, others might say that the person who was responsible for the difficulties my family went through after my disclosure was Jerry Sandusky and him alone. Rationally, I know that is true. I did not ask to be sexually victimized by him. Had he left me alone in that way, there would have been no disclosure; there would have been nothing to disclose; there would have been no sensational case endlessly looping throughout the media.

Still, I made the choice to disclose, and I could have chosen differently. My wife reassures me every day that she would not have wanted it any other way and that the truth has truly set us all free. Yet to me, my wife and children are innocent of all involvement, and yet they have been attacked and ridiculed. I am truly sorry for that. I guess, in some ways, they are also Jerry's victims, just in a much more indirect way.

It was a painful process disclosing to the authorities. It was even more painful dealing with everything once my disclosure was leaked to the media. Everyone, it seemed, had an opinion and not many of those were supportive towards my family, or towards myself. Nor were those people very well informed. They did not understand how child sex offenders groom their victims. They did not understand how it happens gradually, to a confused kid who doesn't even understand what sex is. The shame and the wanting to clam up about it, to put it away in a compartment of your brain, and lock the key to that dark place forever—all that was incomprehensible to them. The way a victim dissociates and denies was foreign to them. They just didn't understand. Yet that didn't stop them from proclaiming their outrageous and hurtful opinions.

What was more, there was an incredible outpouring of support for Jerry. Happy Valley was not so happy about all this. People were up in arms. Sometimes they attacked the victims, saying that we were lying, we were just out for money, saying that we were in cahoots with one another and that we were just trying to hurt a good man.

Frankly, it was like being victimized all over again. The truth does set us free—but it sure can set off a firestorm before doing so.

WE ALL DISCLOSED THE SAME STORY

Fortunately, the similarities of the victims' testimony in the Jerry Sandusky case added to their credibility. Most of the victims didn't know one another. None of them talked together about what had happened to them. I was the only one exposed to one of the victims' stories before coming forward with my own. Yet we all told the same story.   Some would speculate that we all went to the same attorney, or that our attorneys conspired together to coordinate our testimony, but that is not true at all. Yes, I had heard Victim # 4's testimony, and it laid out a course of manipulation and sexual victimization that was strikingly similar to what Jerry had done to me, but it only made me realize that Jerry had a well-tested and successful methodology for grooming boys, and we had both been victims of that grooming. People can speculate all they want but it doesn't change the fact that Jerry Sandusky molested dozens of boys over the course of several decades. Those are just the ones who eventually came forward. Statistically, there is a high likelihood that there are many more victims out there who are still stuck in that conspiracy of silence. I hope some of them read this book and understand that we are all with you. We are all here to support you and show you the way to recovery.

During a boy's first year at The Second Mile, he generally suffered no victimization and was not approached by Jerry. Perhaps during a child's first year at the summer camp the victim was undergoing the initial stages of Jerry's selection process. In any case, the Grand Jury's investigative report recommending charges said that it was typical of Jerry's victims that they were approached during their second year at The Second Mile.[15] This was true in my case as well.

The victims were approached by Jerry at some point in a more personal way than the way most campers interacted with him. This more often than not involved an invitation to a Penn State game as Jerry's guest. If Jerry picked the boy up to drive him there, then Jerry would start by putting a hand on the boy's knee or the thigh as Jerry drove the car. Then there was the tailgate party with the Sandusky family; the fun, the invitations to the Sandusky home and the overnights. There were overnights in hotels during the trips to bowl games. There were gifts of athletic equipment, athletic clothing, expensive shoes, and other items. These great things were then followed by the wrestling matches, soap fights, handling, fondling and sexual assault in the deserted locker and shower rooms of Penn State. There was the "goodnight" fondling when the boy was sleeping over in Sandusky's basement or in my case the upstairs bedrooms. Every victim told virtually the same story with only minor differing details. Details related to their individual lives, vulnerabilities and needs. The

---

15 Report of the Thirty-Third Statewide Investigating Grand Jury, 2011. Available online at http://www.washingtonpost.com/wp-srv/sports/documents/sandusky-grand-jury-report11052011.html.

other victims did not know the stories of the rest of the victims as they recounted these classic grooming and victimization techniques.

There were eight known victims in all cited in the Grand Jury's investigative report. It is likely that there were many more. In fact, a total of 26 verified victims came forward in civil suits against Penn State and Jerry Sandusky. At the time, these were the only eight investigators could find, and Victim Number 8 was never found. The few they found were the only ones willing to come forward and say what Jerry had done to them. They were the only ones ready to wield the power and bear the perils of disclosure, and most of them needed a lot of convincing first.

The day I disclosed to the authorities, I joined the victim's roster. I joined them in their courage and also in all the persecution that was heaped on their heads and the heads of those who were close to them. I have been standing with victims of child sex crimes ever since.

In addition to what happened to Jerry because of my willingness to testify against him, my disclosure itself changed my life irrevocably. It was a fiery rebirth into a new life that had dimensions I couldn't even imagine beforehand. I faced perils and pains I had not dreamed could exist. At the same time that it held perils for me, though, disclosure was an incredibly powerful step towards my recovery.

I firmly believe that it is when he or she discloses that a person begins the long but rewarding journey from being a victim to being a survivor.

Chapter Thirteen:

Healing Begins

I did not have to get on the witness stand and testify after all. Jerry and his lawyers made a strategic decision to keep him off the stand so he would not testify on his own behalf.

Once a defendant takes the stand and makes a claim that the evidence or testimony the prosecutor already put in on the direct case is false or misleading, the prosecutor is then allowed to put on rebuttal witnesses to further prove the truthfulness or accuracy of the evidence originally presented. In this case, I would have been called to rebut Jerry's assertion that he did not molest any boys. By not putting Jerry on the stand, they prevented the prosecutor from putting me on the stand. It became a wash at that point, but knowing Jerry and how "aw, shucks" convincing he is, he might very well have swayed some of the jurors if he had taken the stand to testify. So, in the end, I and my "threatened" testimony really did help gain the conviction. It seems they completely folded up their tents on that one. Experts said it was the pivotal point of the case. The tide turned against Jerry at that point: the point at which I was ready to speak the truth about him in open court.

For my part, though, I had a lot to do besides worry about Jerry's fate. I was busy searching for a therapist to help me start to process, for the first time in my life, the sexual victimization I had suffered at the hands of my adopted father. I had a series of deep emotional wounds I had exposed for the first time, and the aftermath of that was overwhelming. I needed professional help to begin to heal.

I went to weekly meetings with a therapist, and as I spoke, he would nod his head as if he knew what I was talking about. When I would stop speaking, he would just stare at me; then he would ask a question and go back to nodding his head as I spoke.

While it felt good to finally put into words what had happened to me as a child, I didn't feel this particular therapist was able to help me through it. Being listened to helped, yes, but I expected more help with processing what I was bringing out into the light—all the ugly and frightening things Jerry had done to violate not only my body but my soul. It is important to remember, not all therapists are created equal. You have to find one who is both qualified to treat you and who's methodologies and personality mesh with yours. Remember that it is totally your choice.

If you have ever given others raw revelations about yourself, you know you need special support and aid in recovering from that. You are extremely vulnerable during and after such exposure, and you need to be treated with expert care.

For me, I felt as though I was sinking in quicksand after my disclosure. I couldn't find a way out of the morass I found myself in. All I could think about was the victimization. The more I tried to block it out, the more visuals I would see. I had denied it for so long that now that I was owning up to it, the memories flooded over me. I had spent most of my life blocking out or dissociating from the victimization and now I was unable to make it go away.

I'd like to take this opportunity to distinguish my case from those in which people have no recollection about being molested, but then, through "recovered memory" therapy, they "remember" that they were victims. I, on the other hand, tried hard all of my life not to think about the victimization I suffered at the hands of Jerry Sandusky, but I was unsuccessful at doing that. I never "forgot" that Jerry Sandusky molested me. I never lost track of the effects that victimization was having on my life. I simply did not want anyone else in the world to learn what happened to me. Consequently, I did my very best to try to put it out of my mind and go on living my life. Eventually, due to the circumstances, I found that this was something I simply could not do any more. That was the watershed moment in which I knew I had the strength and the courage to disclose the truth about Jerry Sandusky. And that is exactly what I did.

Aaron Fisher also speaks of how his nightmares increased after the victimization stopped and he began to process things with his therapist. "I guess that's because I said out loud what the truth was and the truth was a nightmare," he says in Silent No More. There is that element. You are looking at how bad it really was for the first time, unpeeling the layers of denial. It is one of those sicknesses that gets worse before it gets better. Many victims experience this same phenomenon. During therapy they find their nerves are more raw, their emotions are more tumultuous, and their progress seems to be stilted. This is just the process. Therapy is not an instant fix, and recovery can be a long and hilly road, but this is a necessary journey if you are going to take back your life and go on to live life to the fullest.

I told my wife what was happening and what the therapy sessions were like. She then suggested to me that I might need to seek out a more specialized therapist: one who would know how to get me through what was happening.

That turned out to be one of the best suggestions offered to me during my healing journey. I was fortunate enough to find a very skilled trauma therapist. This is important because most child sex crimes victims are traumatized. Like me, they may have a form of Post Traumatic Stress Disorder and a case of arrested development as well. We have nightmares; we relive the events mentally over and over again; we re-experience the pain, the shame, the powerlessness, and the fear. Some of Jerry's victims say they still glance over their shoulders, even now that he is in prison, feeling like he will loom up behind them. Even from prison, Jerry's crimes exercise this kind of power over the minds and hearts of his victims.

My therapist to this day has not once asked me to tell her the details of what Jerry did to me. She has allowed me to set the pace, but all along the way she has been working with me to teach me new skills to deal with the victimization and its negative effects on my life.

BOUNDARY WORK

One of the very first skills I learned was about boundaries.

Everyone can benefit from learning more about boundaries: their own and others'.

Appropriate boundaries help relationships. They help the individual have more self-respect and they help the individual assert that they expect respect from others. It is also a course in learning to understand and accept the boundaries of others too.

As a child who was physically, mentally, and sexually victimized I was taught that my boundaries were not important; they could be violated with impunity. Children live in a land of giants, so to speak, and more often than not they are given the message that what they think and feel can be over-ridden by adults. They are taught to listen to the big people at all costs. You keep your mouth shut and you don't create waves, because you have no power and you know it.

As I grew from a small child into a young teen, I had no idea what boundaries there should be for myself or others. Because of that I started to cross other people's boundaries without any concern for their well-being. It only intensified as I grew older, persisting throughout my teens and into my twenties. It wasn't until I started therapy that I started to understand not only the damage that had been done to me but also the damage I had done to others. Boundary work has allowed me to start to understand that what I feel and think is significant, and that respecting the personal space and feelings of others is just as important.

Boundary work helped me get through the very difficult period after my disclosure. Everyone was attacking me. There was a radio DJ who would put me on blast every day. He ridiculed me relentlessly and called me a liar. This was a man who had never met me or even tried to speak with me to get some of my perspective, but he spoke with such certainty and dogmatism that

I was everything he was saying I was. It was very painful. It was re-victimization, just like so many other victims of sexual assault or other kinds of victimization undergo.

Sometimes authorities, who are there to protect the victim, wind up hurting the victim all over again. Dr. Weizman recounts in her book about domestic abuse against upscale wives that policemen escorting a beaten woman from her home to protect her treated her like a poor little rich girl—as if her bruises and broken bones hurt any less just because she wore a Calvin Klein outfit to the hospital.

In the days before we understood more about rape, for example, it was common for police authorities to assume that the woman had "asked for it" in some way. It was common for the victim's past to be put on trial in the court. That's another reason why so many crimes of a sexual nature go unreported. Victims have been traumatized enough. They do not need to be disbelieved, mocked, or told they are somehow to blame for what was done to them. They see time and again that these may be the results if they "tell."

Society is growing in understanding about these kinds of crimes, but we have a long, long way to go yet. Part of my work involves educating people about child sexual victimization so we can address it more effectively and compassionately.

The radio DJ wasn't the only person who persecuted me, of course, but he was one of the more public ones. I received a very clear message from this that there are some very cruel individuals in this world who are just waiting to kick others when they are down, blaming suffering people for their own difficulties. That's the easy thing to do. The harder thing to do is to extend a hand and help the person get up, to be a friend to the person who is down. I guess everyone is afraid that compassion will make them vulnerable somehow, so they close off their hearts to the victims, afraid of being "suckered" into supporting them.

Boundaries allowed me to understand that I am in control of what I take in. It was especially important to me because of the high profile case and the last name I carried. My disclosure became fodder for the media just hours after I made it. No one else's testimony was mishandled that way.

Yet I also learned from the experience that I can choose what I allow to affect me. I think of it like a knight in a full suit of armor that has a plate that opens in the chest. The armor is your boundaries, and when something is said or done to you, you have the option to open the plate and let it in or not. You have to determine whether what the person is saying is true or not, whether you need to take it in to change yourself for the better or whether it is untrue and unkind. You also have to decide whether you are going to accept responsibility or not if someone crossed your boundaries; you learn to know where your responsibility begins and ends.

Boundary work was the beginning of my understanding that as an adult I actually do have the control that was taken from me so long ago. I have more power than I had as a child, and I can create and enforce the boundaries I choose.

I think about my boundaries every day, and I try to be cognizant of others' boundaries as well. Respect is a huge boundary we all must have for ourselves and for others. We must respect each other and understand that we all need a helping hand at times.

WORTH

We all want to know that we are being heard. Unfortunately, survivors of child sexual victimization (CSV) go through a large portion of our lives not only feeling as though we are not heard but that what we have to say doesn't matter. When we do get the courage to disclose—and it takes a great deal of courage—we should never be shut down. If we are, though, we have to rise up again and decide that what we have to say does matter, even if no one wants to hear about it or to believe it.

Thus, another key component in my healing journey was to understand that I do matter and I am worthy of a good life. I was beaten down and thought of myself as a bad kid and a worthless person. It was all that I was ever told; that was what my background told me about myself. What's more, Jerry's controlling nature, the way he made me feel valuable through his grooming of me, and then took what he wanted from me. He also interfered with my development of a sense of true self worth. To have a good life, with nice things and cool events and the respect of the community because I was Jerry's boy, I had to endure the sexual victimization. That was a strong message that I was not worthy of a good life unless I paid that price.

I took that message in, and it became a seed that grew with its roots deeply implanted in my entire being. It was not something that was easy to turn around.

As human beings we are all entitled to live joyous and fulfilling lives. Because an individual took advantage of me at a young age, that did not change the fact that I deserved a good childhood without having to submit to sexual victimization. It has been a fight, and I still battle feelings of being unworthy to this day.

Self-love is a key component of every healing journey. It wasn't until I could start to love myself and take care of my own internal thoughts that I could start to truly love others and accept that they truly loved me.

THE GENESIS OF PEACEFUL HEARTS

From the beginning of my disclosure, my wife and I started to look for help. She wanted to find something that would help her learn how she could help me get through my pain and also help her endure the pain she herself was feeling on my behalf. The high profile nature of the case, the accusations from the DJ and others, all affected her too. We were two people struggling through one of the toughest moments of our lives, and help was not readily available.

I was looking for a Twelve Step program of some sort to get me through, but what I was really looking for was to hear from someone who had been through it too. I needed to interact with someone who could tell me that I wasn't alone and that what I was feeling and thinking was normal for my stage of healing.

What we learned was that there wasn't much help like that available. It was during this time that we brainstormed an idea. If we couldn't find the help we needed, we would create it ourselves. The Peaceful Hearts Foundation was our answer.

The Peaceful Hearts Foundation was created from our pain. We established it with the idea to help others so they would never have to get to a space of feeling as alone and helpless as we did. We did feel very alone. Family, friends, and colleagues turned their backs on us, not because we did anything wrong, but because they couldn't comprehend what we were going through. All of those people, whether they meant to or not, kicked us when we were down. There were a few people who stayed around and these were true friends, but there were very few. Peaceful Hearts was started with the simple idea of helping others like ourselves. We didn't know how we were going to do it, but we knew that nobody should ever have to feel like we did at that time.

Along with working on myself through therapy over the next two years, I took on the task of educating myself on the issue of child sexual victimization. While I had the direct firsthand experience of having been sexually victimized as a child, I had very little knowledge of the issue itself. Therapy teaches me how to work on myself and take control of my life, but educating myself on the issue has taught me how many people are suffering out there, how child sexual victimization may be prevented, and how to help others going through it. I have learned about how to recognize it, how to disclose, and how to respond when someone discloses to you. By working on myself and educating myself on the issue, I have found that healing can and will happen. Knowledge is definitely power.

Being sexually victimized is not a death sentence. You can and will overcome the victimization. It may not be easy, and all the work will be placed directly on your shoulders, which may seem unfair, but you can also look at it as a blessing in disguise.

You will be happier and healthier after all this work, because you will learn things not only about being a survivor of child sexual victimization but about life itself and how to live a good one. What is more, research shows that males who are victimized as boys develop more empathy for others as they grow up. This makes sense when you take into account that they know exactly what it feels like to suffer, they understand it, and they want to alleviate that suffering in others. So, victims of child sexual victimization can make the transition from wounded to being healers themselves, equipped with an extra store of empathy for others' pain.

I can tell you that in the end, it is so worth it to face it head on and work your way through it, however slowly and painfully that might be. You cannot overcome it until you do. It will be with you until you expose it. It will seep into everything you think and do until you face it and make your way through to the other side.

I finally made the decision to run into the pain and fear instead of running away from it. It has been one of the best decisions I have ever made. Although I discovered all too well the perils of disclosure, I also discovered its tremendous healing power and the power of truth in liberating the human spirit. The Peaceful Hearts Foundation is part of that healing journey, and I devoutly hope it will serve as a forum for others to heal too.

CHAPTER FOURTEEN:

Oprah's Calling...

S hortly after my disclosure to the police was leaked to the media, I started receiving requests to do sit-down interviews. At the time I was in no place to sit down and talk about what I had gone through in any kind of a public way. I was trying to come to terms with my own victimization and the fact that my entire family had abandoned me and had in addition accused me of lying and of pursuing financial interests only. I also was coming to terms with the fact that the world now knew about the things that were done to me and the things I was forced to do. I was coping with a lot.

Survivors of child sexual victimization who disclose always need to deal with a lot of issues, but mine had to be played out in the public eye because of the high profile nature of the case. That added to the pressure and pain. Even the fact that my private conference with law enforcement and attorneys became public was a challenge I had not realized I would have to face. In a less famous case, with a less famous name, it never would have happened. This had been the first time I ever went before an authority and disclosed the fact that Jerry victimized me; it was the first time I trusted them enough or had the strength, courage, and determination to seek justice for what Jerry had done to me. To have my private words being bandied about on television as the latest sensation was wounding, to say the least.

What was more, I had a wife and children to protect. I had to try to shield them not only from the agonies of the disclosure itself, but from the media circus that surrounded the whole case. Some of the bright lights and microphones of the media were aimed at them, and yet they'd had nothing to do with any of it. It was painful to see their privacy being invaded like that.

For all of these reasons, I did not accept any invitations for interviews. I had much work to do before I would be ready to talk about being victimized in the public eye, if I would ever be able to do so. I think it was a very wise decision for the particular stage of healing I was at during that time.

I spent the next two years in therapy with a specialized trauma therapist. I was working hard to understand how badly the victimization had affected my life and trying to repair what I could. I had plenty of internal work on my hands to keep me busy for a long, long time. Yet an opportunity came along that I simply could not let pass by, and the timing seemed right as well.

A Life-Changing Opportunity

I received a call from my lawyer one day. She asked me if I would be interested in speaking with a producer from Oprah Winfrey's television network OWN. By this time I felt as though I was ready to at least have a conversation with a media representative about what they were looking for from me. I placed a call to the producer, but I was wary and mistrustful of him and his motives. I did not want my story to be exploited by any more media, and these were the big leagues. I introduced myself over the phone, and we spoke for about an hour. This was a very good conversation. There was no pressure, no sense of being used. We really just got to know each other a little bit. He told me he would call me back in about a week after he spoke with some of his people.

When he called the next week he told me that everyone, including Oprah, was very excited at the possibility of having me sit down to do an interview about my relationship with Jerry and how he had taken advantage of me sexually. Frankly, I couldn't believe what he was saying. Oprah Winfrey!

I knew that, as a survivor of child sexual victimization herself, Oprah had empowered survivors everywhere not to be silenced or ashamed. She has been an inspiration for millions. She is someone who struggled and overcame abuse in her life to become a source of strength and hope for others.

She was also someone that I admired and looked up to, but I never really thought I could get to where she was in her healing. I also never dreamed I would get to talk to her in person.

When Oprah was but nine years old, an older cousin who was nineteen years old forced sex upon her. As is so often the case, her offender was a trusted person, a member of her extended family. As is also so often the case, the cousin told her not to tell anyone. He took her out for ice cream afterward. In the most usual way of victims of child sex crimes, she stayed silent about the victimization. She also endured and stayed silent about the victimization that was to come later from a family friend and an uncle. (The sad fact is that once a child is sexually victimized by one offender, they run a much higher risk of being victimized by others.)

Oprah understood from personal experience the shame and the silence of the child sexual victimization victim. One of her documentaries about child sexual victimization is entitled "Scared Silent," which describes the case of so many victims, who also may love and depend on the perpetrators even as they hate the victimization. Oprah understood too that acting out is sometimes the only way victims of child sex crimes have to express their frustration and pain.

I felt she was someone who could understand me, and she did. We laughed together during the interview about the typical view of the child molester as a man in a van, when in fact it is so often a family member or close family friend.

I learned that it wasn't the money or fame that helped Oprah heal; it was the light within her. She let it shine and it destroyed the darkness. The fame and money were byproducts of her being who she was truly meant to be. I learned that we all have a light inside, and if we choose to let it shine, we too can heal and be inspirations to the world.

WHEN OPPORTUNITY KNOCKS . . .

As the producer and I spoke more and more, trust grew, and we eventually worked out a date to shoot the interview. The producer, Chad, made a lot of promises to me in order to win my trust and not one of them was financial. I was not paid to do the interview. I was not promised anything of a promotional nature. I was treated with care, respect, and belief, and those intangibles are worth more than any amount of money.

My motives for doing the interview were simple: I wanted to tell the truth, and I wanted to put a face on an epidemic that society is still struggling to bring to the surface and into the national conversation. I had the opportunity to do this because Jerry Sandusky and his crimes were so infamous. Because I bore his name as his adopted son, forums would open to me that would not open to other survivors, so I thought it was important to accept this opportunity to speak out. I thought that if I went to the interview and answered every question honestly, no matter what was asked, I couldn't fail. I wanted to give the audience a look into the life of a survivor of child sexual victimization from a person the media really wanted to pay attention to: Jerry Sandusky's adopted son.

Finally the time arrived to fly to Chicago to film the interview. I was excited and I felt ready for this experience. I knew it was a huge step in my healing journey. While I slept better than I had in awhile, my wife did not. She is my worrier, and she gets nervous for me. That is one of the many reasons why I love her. She couldn't believe that I was able to sleep so well the night before not only meeting Oprah Winfrey but also going on television with her in front of her massive world audience and disclosing my victimization. It would most likely be the largest audience I would ever get to address. This was huge, and my wife was anxious. At the same time, she was glad and proud.

The car showed up and picked us up at our hotel. We were driven to Harpo Studios. Once inside we had to wait for Chad to come and get us. He then took us out to see the set and then to the green room for hair and makeup. It was so exciting, walking down the hallway with pictures of the hundreds of celebrities Oprah had interviewed over the years and to be in the same place she was.

For many years Oprah had used her show as a platform to discuss child sexual victimization. Since she herself was a survivor, she allowed many others to come on the show to join in the conversation and to disclose their truths. I watched a show that Oprah did with two hundred male survivors (including Jim Clemente), and it was one of the most emotional experiences that I have ever witnessed on a television show. So many men were shedding their shame and guilt to come forward and say, "I am a survivor of childhood sexual victimization." The courage showed by those men inspired me. This is one of the beautiful things survivors give to one another: the courage to come forward. It was the gift Victim Number 4 gave to me, and I will never forget it. I try to pay it back every day by giving that same gift to other survivors, and I am grateful to all those who have the inner strength to come forward.

When it came time for the interview, I was taken out on the stage and given a chair. I was alone for a few minutes, minus all the cameras and sound people, and I remember thinking, "This can't be real." Then I heard that famous voice. The first words I heard spoken to me by Oprah were, " I just met your spawn back there. I swear he looks just like you." With this casual little joke, she had broken the ice and I was ready. The little bit of pressure I was feeling melted away as we sat together for the next two hours and discussed the victimization I had suffered at the hands of my adoptive father to a fellow survivor. I couldn't believe how quickly time flew by. Oprah is such a skilled questioner and excellent listener. She is so present to the person she is interviewing; her facial expressions, her eyes, and her body posture all communicate "I'm with you." It was not hard to open up to Oprah. When I was finished, Oprah simply said, "Great job."

The first question Oprah asked me on stage was how I first met Jerry Sandusky, and I replied that I had met him at The

Second Mile, when I was about eight years old. I described the evenings when he would meet with us, and we would play games and he would make jokes. She quoted from Jerry's book *Touched*, which she found an ironic title. She read Jerry's words recounting meeting me: "Matt became an instant challenge for me. I didn't want to see him go through life by himself at such a young age, I didn't want to lose him to whatever fates might have awaited him, so I kept trying and trying to pull him in." She found that an unintentional revealing of Jerry's real motive: "to pull him in" and "touched." She mentioned that in her mind, the stories about Jerry Sandusky showed the "true face" of classic sexual grooming and victimization: that is not the face of a monster, but the kindly face of a trusted friend.

We laughed together about the stereotypes of the bogeyman, the man in the van, but how it is really the people who are closest to you who are "the master manipulators," as she termed them. She asked me when Jerry's manipulation of me started, and I replied that it started from the very beginning; from the moment he first met me. That was when he started the grooming process, picking me out of hundreds of kids.

She mentioned that a child at that age, without any sexual experience, didn't have the language to express what the person was doing. I could only use the word "awkward" to describe my feelings about those times with Jerry, and she understood.

EXPLORING NEW DEPTHS WITH OPRAH

Oprah is so empathic, I was able to tell her how I wanted him off me when he would lay on top of me, and that I knew it wasn't right, and that I didn't want it, but that I felt helpless and that I felt I had to take it. She asked me insightfully if I had felt I had to take it in order to have a "dad" type figure in my life, and I said I had felt that way, yes. I told of how the overnight visits were good except for the one bad part, the bedtime ritual. I said that looking around the Sandusky home on those occasions, before bedtime, I had always wished I could have a family like that one. I had wished I had a mother who cooked dinner every night for the whole family, and I wished that I had brothers and sisters who cared for me like that. "Ninety percent of the time with Jerry Sandusky was everything that a child would want," I told her. "He gave you things. You had fun. You went places that you would never go without him. But the 10 percent of the time where he was doing these things? It can't even compare. That 90 percent—it gets obliterated by the damage that is done to you." I noted that the victim may be compliant during those times, allowing the offender his time because it doesn't seem worth it to cause an issue or upset the person. You endure, but after a while, the 90 percent isn't worth it any more, on any terms, especially as you mature and begin to understand what the offender is really doing to you.

We touched on how sexual victimization may not be painful. I said I didn't want to say it was pleasurable, but that it wasn't the most painful thing. Oprah implied that it was okay to say it was pleasurable at times, because our bodies betray us. Genital arousal is a biological reality; it happens when certain things are done to the body. Oprah has been praised by doctors dealing with child sexual victimization by being willing to say that "involuntary physical sexual arousal is often an aspect of sexual victimization" and is indeed a "powerful tool" used by sexual predators to shame their victims into silence.16 The victims feel complicit because their bodies betray them. This is part of the sorry snare the child gets trapped in and reinforces the decisions not to tell anyone.

She asked me when I first decided I was going to speak up, and I talked about the big wall mirror in our bathroom and how I looked at myself in the mirror after Victim Number 4's testimony and asked myself, "What am I going to do?" Was I going to keep my mouth shut? If I kept my mouth shut, I would be protected. I would have nothing to worry about. Or was I going

16 Janet Rosenzweig, MS, PhD, MPA, Lessons from Oprah's interview with Matt Sandusky,http://www.philly.com/philly/blogs/healthy_kids/Lessons-from-Oprah-Winfreys-interview-with-Matt-Sandusky.html. Posted: Wednesday, July 30, 2014, 10:31 AM

to do the right thing, the hard thing, and go to the Attorney General's office and tell him I was sexually victimized as a child?" I mentioned how "I had to take everything in. I was married. That was going to impact my wife, my children. It would have been better for me to have kept it to myself, to have carried it myself. I truly believe it would have been better." She asked me if I felt that way even now, and I almost broke down. "Yes," I said, "because I can handle it. I can handle people attacking me. I handled the victimization. I can take it. My wife, is an innocent, my children, they're innocent, and for people to attack them . . . Absolutely, the simpler answer would be for me to keep it, to deal with it on my own, to never tell anybody, to be by myself with it."

"But you didn't," Oprah said with the faintest of smiles, as if reinforcing my decision and seeming to compliment me with her eyes. "You came forward. And I read that you came forward because you didn't want to be a coward."

"That was the choice as I saw it," I told her. "Yes. I felt I had been a coward up to that point. I had numerous opportunities to tell people. I had numerous opportunities to tell law enforcement, and I didn't." I added that one of the main reasons I never told on Jerry was because "I was afraid of that man."

Oprah mentioned that Penn State paid out $60 million dollars to Jerry's victims, and she said that people might think I disclosed the victimization for the money. I explained that I did not know that they were making any pay-outs at the time, and that was not my motivation for speaking out. She asked me how the audience could be sure I was telling the truth. I explained that there would be no reason for me to subject my wife and children to the kinds of attacks they had undergone and would undergo even from me coming on national television with her if I were not telling the truth. I would certainly not put the people I love through that for the sake of money. There was only one reason I had to disclose and it was to help, myself and anyone else who has been sexually victimized.

What Price for a Child's Soul?

I just want to pause for a moment on the idea of financial restitution for victims of child sex crimes. In fact, no amount of money can ever restore what happens to a child's psyche in a child sexual victimization case.

Nature bestows on us certain gifts. Those gifts cannot be replaced by money. One of those gifts is the innocence of children. Money cannot buy that back once it has been taken from a child. A return to innocence requires deep restoration of the soul. It comes from healing done through intense internal work, which is largely up to the individual and cannot be bought even with the most expensive therapist. Money may ease the pressures and stresses of life financially so that a survivor can concentrate more on healing, and in that way, financial restitution can be very helpful. But it can never buy back what was lost; it can never unbreak that which was broken. Only deep healing can do that.

There really are some things in life that money just can't buy. The wholeness of a child's psyche is one of those things.

Catharsis

Meeting Oprah and being on her show, interviewed before millions of people and disclosing my victimization so publicly was a cathartic experience for me. My wife joined Oprah and I on stage and we all took some pictures together. It was a moment that I will always cherish. It happened because I took a risk and made myself vulnerable. I took the risk in order to help others heal, but it was a huge step forward in my own healing journey as well.

Oprah, Kim and I also talked off camera for about thirty minutes. Those thirty minutes have been some of the most influential in my process to date. Oprah warned me that people would attack me for doing the interview and to be prepared for that. She said, "Do not worry about those people; they are not who you are trying to reach. Going forward you have to decide about everything, does it add value to what you are doing?" This is something I think about every day since that interview. I look at everything and everyone and I ask the question: "Does this/they add value to what I'm doing?" and if it or they do not I let it/them go. It is a great boundaries exercise, and it makes things very clear.

When the time came for the show to air, I was more nervous to watch it than I had been to actually sit down and do the interview. By the time the show concluded that first hour, our Inbox started filling with people reaching out and disclosing their own victimization and others sending their kind words of support. This same thing would happen every time the show aired and new people would catch the episode. There are so many people hurting in this world, and they feel alone. My goal was to do the interview and have each and every one of them know that they are not alone. I wanted them to experience the catharsis of coming forward too.

By doing the Oprah interview and speaking with her personally, my mission became clearer. It is to be a voice for the voiceless. It is to show survivors everywhere that they no longer need to be silenced or ashamed of what happened to them as children. It is to make sure every survivor knows that within him or her there is a light and that person alone has the power to let it shine. That is the gift a person gives to the world, and it holds true for all of us. By letting our lights shine, we are empowering others to do the same. I can think of no greater gift to give.

Hopefully, the interview also serves educational purposes about child sexual victimization by dispelling some of the myths about it and giving it a personality and a face. One commentator said that the interview was like a seminar in child sexual victimization. I am happy to give such seminars if they can serve in a preventive capacity to save even one child from the kinds of things I went through.

I want to thank Oprah for encouraging me to stay focused and for being an inspiration to not only survivors of child sexual victimization but truly to all of humankind. Being on her show and receiving the response I did made me realize how important my disclosure was in order to help people come to grips with what had happened to them. People like Oprah make it all worthwhile.

CHAPTER FIFTEEN:

Lessons Learned

In the course of my long journey toward the truth, I have learned some lessons I believe are valuable to everyone, including and especially survivors of child sexual victimization. I hope the reader finds these insights useful, comforting, and restorative. For those readers who are not survivors of one form of victimization or another, I believe there is something to be learned from my experience about human healing in general. Many of us have trauma we need to recover from. Many of the lessons learned in healing from trauma apply to all kinds of tragic losses.

Elaine Marshall once said "healing is not the same as being cured. A cure is quick, clean, and over and done with. Healing is often a lifelong process of recovery and growth. Cure is passive, and healing is active. We must be awake, aware, and participating as healing happens, and it happens over time. It usually proceeds in stages, and these stages may not be orderly or progressive."[17] Sometimes you have to go back a few steps before you can go forward when it comes to healing, but if you stay the course, healing will happen. This applies to every kind of healing, whether it be physical, mental, emotional, or spiritual.

Some of Jerry's victims are clearly still healing. For example, one of Jerry Sandusky's victims, Victim #1 (Aaron Fisher) says in his book Silent No More that to this day he checks the back seat and trunk of his car before getting in. He just feels a sense of vague threat. He dislikes sleeping in a bed, because of all that was done to him in beds. His psychologist noted that Aaron still doesn't really like to be touched, except by his girlfriend. He is still healing. There are still places in his psyche that are sensitive

---

17 Elaine S. Marshall, "Learning the Healer's Art," BYU devotional address, 8 October 2002.

and hurting. Trauma can take a long time to get over. There is no instant cure.

At the same time, child sexual victimization survivors should be aware that they can and will heal. There should be no doubt about that, no matter how awful everyone says your situation may be. Look at Oprah if you want to see an example of a survivor who has progressed so far in her own healing she is able to help others on their journey. In fact, for many survivors, helping others is an important part of their own recovery. Oprah is one of the most successful people on Earth, on many levels. She is an example of how child sexual victimization survivors can overcome and go on to live great lives.

Don't let frightening words about what happened to you frighten you off or make you think there is no hope for your healing. As retired FBI agent Jim Clemente said in his report, sometimes the language used to describe child sexual victimization is what a journalist might refer to as purple prose. To express their great moral indignation, people will talk about how a Jerry Sandusky "ruined lives" or "devastated children" or performed "hideous, heinous acts" upon children. It's true; he did. That doesn't mean those things cannot be overcome, though. Let's not be stopped by the language applied by people who only mean to express their moral indignation over these people's actions.

As I quoted in the previous chapter, a psychologist talked about child sexual victimization being "emotional homicide" and "murder of the soul." Yet survivors do not want to hear that they have been murdered emotionally and spiritually, or that their lives were irredeemably ruined, broken, hideously scarred, et cetera. A child sexual victimization survivor should not feel like he or she has been through something that will leave him or her forever defective, crippled, destroyed, and permanently scarred. That simply isn't so. People can and do recover from child sexual victimization. They become whole. Their lives are re-constructed into something stronger and more resilient than ever before.

As the old saying goes, it is the torn fabric that has been mended that is the strongest. Many people have experienced similar traumas, or worse, and they have gone on to live worthy and satisfied lives. It may help to read the life stories of survivors of the Holocaust, for example. After enduring inhuman suffering, many of them went on to build happy marriages, good families, successful businesses, and lives of satisfaction. As I said in an earlier chapter, the human spirit is the ultimate survivor.

Child sexual victimization survivors should never feel that they have been so damaged that they can't recover. In fact, the opposite is true. The fact that they survived the crimes committed against them means that they have proven their strength and resilience and have the tools and an opportunity to thrive. As previously mentioned, it will take some time, and it is important to be kind to yourself and patient as well. Overnight cures don't exist. It also will take some courage. The survivor must actively take part in facing all of his or her particular realities. It will happen, however, because the human spirit is indomitable and redeemable. It will happen because no secret is so deep and dark that the sunshine of truth can't reveal it and disinfect it. No wound is so deep that love can't filter into it and restore it to wholeness.

MY FIRST STEP: RECOGNIZE AND ACKNOWLEDGE

My first step in beginning the healing journey was to recognize and acknowledge that I was victimized and that it matters. I could see through Jerry's criminal trial that it matters to society too. For the first time in my life I saw society's authorities lining up on my side and telling me that my victimization mattered. I saw that people were upset by what Jerry had done to children, including me. I learned that it was illegal for a person to be violated the way Jerry violated me.

Sometimes the survivor does not have that gratification and reinforcement, though. Sometimes we have to assert it within ourselves without back up. Perpetrators may be long gone, and they may never be caught and punished. Survivors sometimes have to live with that reality. However, the most important assertions of self-respect come from inside ourselves. Even without the justice system being able to punish the perpetrators who offended against us, we must know that what was done to us was wrong and that matters. Child sexual victimization is a crime. It is a crime for which Jerry Sandusky is now serving what amounts to a life sentence in prison.

Trauma often undermines a person's self–esteem. As survivors we usually find that we have low self-esteem, and we tend to think that our pain doesn't count for much, as if we deserved what happened to us. We may feel we somehow brought it about. We feel cast aside, especially in cases where society circles the wagons to protect the "nice guy" that victimizes us with disbelief that he could ever do such a thing.

We didn't bring it about. We are not guilty. Our pain counts. Know that.

Yet even acknowledging that the victimization occurred at all is in and of itself difficult. This was one of the hardest parts for me, and it was hard for Jerry's other victims and it is hard for most victims of child sex crimes. Jim Clemente noted in his report that, even when they were specifically asked about the victimization by investigators, none of Jerry's victims admitted to it at first. In fact, most of them flatly denied that anything had happened. It took a lot of time for them to disclose, and sometimes they did it in bits and pieces over a period of time, letting more and more truth out as they found it safe to do so and as they could admit to themselves what had really happened to them. This phenomenon is known as incremental disclosure and it is the norm in child sexual victimization cases.

I didn't want to admit what had happened, because to admit it had really happened would shape the way I saw myself. It would factor into my very self-image and undermine it completely. Yet I also knew that it was real, and the time came that I couldn't deny it any longer. I had to take the steps to break the control it had held over my life for so long. I had to make the decision to face it. I would no longer run from it, no matter how hard or painful the journey to face it down might be. The longest journey begins with the first step, and this first step is admitting that this really did happen to you. There need be no more hiding or running from it, no matter how hard it may be to face. As they say, "When you are going through hell, keep going." You'll come out on the other side.

You may have to grieve some. Child sex crimes victims have suffered real and also intangible losses. Grief, though it is painful to go through, is the natural way to get over a loss. Give yourself permission to grieve. You lost your innocence. You lost parts of your childhood. You lost trust in anyone remotely resembling the offender. Society, your parents, your teachers, and all those who were supposed to protect you may seem ineffectual at preventing your victimization or possibly even complicit in it. It is okay to mourn those losses. This is all part of facing what really happened. It's no fun. Yet until you thoroughly grieve what was taken from you, you will not truly be free of it.

I have always found writing to be a great release. It's a way to get the feelings outside of myself without actually having to sit down in a therapy session or try to explain to someone verbally what you are thinking. Writing has been very empowering for me. I found in my darkest and most fear-filled moments that writing in my journal allowed me to express those feelings and not to have to worry about someone judging me for my words.

I highly recommend journaling. You can always shred or burn the pages if you don't want others to read what you have written. However, writing it all out is a tremendous mental and emotional release. You can scream on the page, and no one will hear you, but you will have gotten your emotions outside of yourself. Paper and pen may wind up being your best friends.

It was through writing that I started to understand that healing was not always going to be linear, always moving forward. It would have its ups and downs, regressions and progressions. Sometime healing may come in spirals that seem to take you back to points you've been before. Yet the general direction of the spiral is upward, toward liberation.

EMBRACE THE JOURNEY—AND THE SETBACKS

I have learned to embrace the journey with all its ups and downs. When things are going well, of course, it's easy to feel good. The journey clips steadily along. But what happens when things don't go as we planned, or when something we tried doesn't work, when we feel we have lost some ground we'd previously gained? We must understand that failure and disappointment are part of the journey, but they are not the journey's end.

Failure is often looked down upon as unfortunate and unwanted. The emotions associated with failure are typically disappointment, shame or anger. But we need to start to view failure as a step, a step that didn't work, nevertheless it is still a necessary step to success. It is a learning opportunity to discover what isn't effective so we can better understand what is. Overcoming failure or setback strengthens us and makes us wiser next time.

We can think of setbacks and failures in many different ways that will help us, not hinder us. One way to think of setbacks is as if you are making, say, a long jump. Before you leap, you'll go back a short distance to give yourself a running start. Think of therapeutic setbacks and failures as you taking some steps back to give yourself a running start so you can take a greater leap forward in your recovery.

In her 2013 commencement address at Harvard, Oprah had something to say about failure. She said there is no such thing! "Failure," she said, "is just life trying to move us in another direction." That's an extremely positive and empowering way to look at failure.

Personally, I have tried many things along my journey, and many of those things have not worked and did not contribute to getting me to the place I am today. I had the choice to quit when they didn't work, but I chose to move on to the next idea. I didn't see it as though I had failed in some way. I saw it as providing me with an awareness of a way that didn't work for me. Instead of being beaten down or feeling sorry for myself, I was inspired to try something else.

We've all heard the story about Thomas Edison and the light bulb. Even though he failed one thousand times to find the proper filament that would work, he did not consider those times failures. They simply provided him with a checklist of what didn't work to make a light bulb. He said something like, "I have not failed to make a light bulb. I have found 999 ways not to make a light bulb." In Edison's mind, he was simply eliminating all the ways that didn't work. No wonder that when this man died, people all over the world dimmed their lights in tribute! In his perseverance and his willingness to "fail and fail again," he gave us a very special kind of light for the spirit too.

I had held a self-defeating mindset for most of my life, always telling myself I was a screw up if I couldn't do something, or feeling as though I was "less than" if I made a mistake or fell short. I had to make the decision to change how I spoke to myself, and that directly related to how I viewed failure. Failure is not a word that I even bother to use anymore. As I stated, it is better to look at a "failure" simply as something that didn't work and not become discouraged.

I knew that nothing was going to change if I threw up my hands and quit. I didn't want anyone feeling sorry for me, and I surely was not going to feel sorry for myself any longer. So I came to see that the only real failure is giving up.

Forgive yourself when you fall short. Everyone has shortcomings and imperfections. Not everything you try is going to work; you won't be good at everything you do; sometimes you are going to make errors. Everyone on this earth makes mistakes; some people make spectacular ones. Yours are probably not as serious as all that. Forgiving yourself is a huge step toward healing. Let up on yourself! You're doing the best that you can, and you always have. There's nothing wrong with a little mercy and compassion directed at you. Give yourself a break. Cut yourself some slack. I am not saying to wallow in self-pity; I am just saying that when you pay attention to your self-talk and you find that it is abusive, you should answer it back with merciful, kind, and loving things about yourself.

This beautiful verse from *The Desiderata* is helpful to some people: "Beyond a wholesome discipline, be gentle with yourself. You are a child of the universe no less than the trees and the stars; you have a right to be here."

I know that in order to heal from childhood sexual victimization or any trauma you must experiment a lot, and in doing so you will fall often before you reach your goals. If we look at each failure simply as a step in the process of healing, a milestone on our way to reaching our dreams instead interpreting them negatively, we will remain encouraged to keep trying. Then we will succeed.

LIFE IS HARD

The next lesson I learned was that life is hard and sometimes it is just plain unfair. I feel that there is no real rhyme or reason for this being true; it just is. By understanding this, I was able to stop feeling sorry for myself. I knew that there would never be a way to stop the twists and turns life was going to throw at me; I could only control how I responded to them. I also saw that the universe didn't have it in for me. God wasn't out to get me! I had lived for a long time thinking that this was what life was about: some people are doomed to a life filled with hardships while others reap all the rewards. I saw myself as one of the doomed. But if you open your eyes and pay attention to the people around you, you'll see there are always people who are less fortunate, and it is important to notice their struggles too. There is always someone who is worse off than you are; someone who experienced more hardship, deprivation, and suffering than you have. Somehow they survived, and you will too. Life is hard for everyone; some more than others, but everyone gets their piece of the action. Sometimes those we think of as having some sort of ideal life turn out to suffer grave misfortune, or we find out they have already suffered grave misfortune in their lives and have overcome it. Life is difficult. It just is.

I realized at one point that I had victim mentality and was blaming everything and everyone else for where I was. Until I decided to take ownership of my life and where I wanted to go, I was destined always to be a victim. I wasn't going to let that happen any longer. I decided to take things on as they came. I decided not to fear what was going to happen but to take each challenge as it crossed my path. In doing so I broke challenges down into smaller parts, manageable steps that were easier to overcome one by one rather than taking them on all together. I was able to see that hardships happen to everyone, because life is indeed hard.

The power to live a joy-filled life is within us all, no matter what our circumstances. We have everything we need to succeed inside of us already. I am not saying that we don't need help, and it is so important to realize that there is no magical cure, but there is a blessing that is inside each of us. All that energy that you've used to protect yourself for so long will be the exact thing that will get you through the pain along your healing journey, once you open up and begin using it that way.

There is an old saying that states, "We would not understand true joy if we didn't at some point feel pain." I am not sure how true that is, but I can tell you that having the courage to face what happened to me, and making the decision not to let it control me any longer, has enabled me to reach a point where I love my life and the person that I am today.

From the first moment I was publicly attacked for my disclosure, I knew that this journey, like life, was not going to be easy. I also knew that once I had committed to healing, I wanted everything I was going to encounter to serve a higher purpose than just getting me better. I hoped it would be something that eventually could empower and assist other survivors of child sexual victimization to start their own journeys and to overcome their own childhood traumas.

It hurt each time I was attacked or ridiculed. Some instances hurt more than others, but it never stopped being painful. Yet it also gave me the opportunity to grow. What I learned was that, perhaps because I had endured so much at the hands of the offender, my armor could take a lot. My family and I took a lot of hits, but each time we were still left standing. Eventually those scars healed, which only renewed my vigor to keep moving forward.

I would tell my wife, "Every time these people attack us, they are only making us stronger and less afraid." I can tell you that every fear a survivor or victim has about disclosing, about coming forward about their victimization, has some basis in reality. It's there; it could actually happen. People may not believe you. They may go so far as to call you a liar. People will try to discredit you. Some people will leave you; some people will avoid you.

Yet when you fight through the fear that is attached to it all, you learn there was never really anything to fear. Fear is something that you create in your mind. What you learn is that you have the power to destroy that fear. You will survive it all. You survived the victimization. You will survive the aftermath too.

Almost like encountering a bully in the schoolyard, sometimes the only answer to the really nasty critics is to rise up and punch them right in the nose. Sometimes it takes that before they finally leave you alone. I don't mean literally, of course. But you can't let the nay-sayers determine what you do. This book represents me standing up and hitting all of those bullies in the nose. I do not fear them or anyone.

I have at times allowed the darkness to engulf me and to extinguish my light, and I realized that eventually if you keep moving forward by fighting through the gloom, the light is reignited and burns brighter than ever before.

STEP OUTSIDE ALL "COMFORT ZONES"

We have to be ready to make ourselves vulnerable if we are ever going to breathe life into our dreams. A large number of people will never realize their dreams because they avoid pain and struggle due to fear of failure. They are content to stay in their comfort zones. Yet a comfort zone is not a place of growth. A comfort zone is where you stagnate.

When we are willing to step outside our comfort zones, we start to face our fears, and in facing our fears, we realize just how insignificant those fears actually are. I am not saying I don't have fears, but I do not let those trepidations stop me from living a fulfilled life. As a survivor of child sexual victimization, I understand the role fear plays in the victimization itself, in preventing disclosure, and in hindering the recovery from the victimization. Fear is paralyzing; it kills hopes and dreams. The real challenge of growth, when you have been beaten down by fear, is to have the courage to start over again. My life has afforded me many opportunities for growth when I could take up the challenge to start over. It has always been well worth it to stand up, dust myself off and try again.

Always remember that the human spirit is indomitable. It is very hard to keep that spirit down for long. It will rise again, like a phoenix. As far as I can tell, the human spirit is the ultimate survivor, and it is inside all of us.

BE RELENTLESS

I have also learned to be relentless in the pursuit of healing. During the process you will endure disappointment, failure, pain, and defeats, but you will learn things about yourself that you didn't know before you started. What you will realize is the greatness we all have within us; that you are more powerful than you ever could have imagined, and that you are worthy. Those concepts are intrinsically intertwined. In fact, once you realize you are actually personally worthy, you will inevitably feel the power and greatness you possess. I have fallen many times throughout my life and during my healing journey, but as I mentioned above,

I am proud to say that I always got back up. I'm asking you to not be deterred from your dreams. The only thing that is guaranteed to stop you from reaching your dreams is you giving them up.

There is nothing more empowering than knowing that anything you dream can and will come true. You have to be willing to put in the work, though. You will have to take your hits and learn to get back up on your feet again. As I said, life is hard and full of struggles. As child sexual victimization survivors we understand some of the intensity of life's struggles very well. A lot of the struggles we face may not be fair, they may not be deserved, we may have done nothing to bring them upon ourselves, but they are still there and we must face them. If we are thrown off course by them, we must learn that the race is not over as long as you have a beating heart and are drawing breath. There is precious time left to muster your strength, focus on the finish line, and hop back on the track. Never, ever give up on your dreams. Be relentless in your pursuit of them. The only person who can defeat you is you.

DEFINE YOUR VALUE

I also think it is important to understand that we alone get to define our value. As survivors we don't have to believe the dogma of what we are supposed to be or how we are supposed to act. We certainly do not have to believe the message the offenders gave us that our minds and our hearts and our wishes didn't matter—and that all that mattered was our bodies' usefulness for their gratification. We are the ones who get to decide who we are and what our value is. We have infinite value as human beings. Our nation's Declaration of Independence notes that every human being, by virtue of being created by God, is worthy of life, liberty, and the pursuit of happiness. Just because these fundamental rights were denied to us by the offenders, that does not mean we have to accept that we are not worthy of these and all other human rights. We *are* worthy of them. We have value.

Don't let other people's opinions of you define who you are. Don't let their words and actions affect how you feel about yourself.

When I first disclosed, my family felt as though we lost a great deal. After all, we lost family members, friends, and we were attacked in a very public way. The Sandusky family turned their backs on me, after years of knowing and loving one another. I was made out to be the bad guy, not Jerry. At the time, I could have started to believe the things people were saying about me. I could have believed that I was no good, only after money, untruthful, and all the things people wanted to accuse me of in order to keep the mythology about Jerry and the Penn State Football program going—the whole Happy Valley legend and Jerry's part in it. I could have taken in those accusations and questioned myself, thinking maybe I was as bad a person as they were saying I was. Yet I knew I was telling the truth and why. That gave me strength.

This is just another example of why you can't let other people's definition of you define who you are. Only you have that power and right.

I also could have held onto the victim label and felt sorry for myself, but honestly, that was never an option. I cannot tell you that it was easy because it was one of the most painful times of my life and my family's. It was definitely not easy. But we knew who we were and that was enough. We picked ourselves back up, and what we realized was that what we thought was loss was actually opportunity. It was the opportunity to choose whom we wanted to surround ourselves with. If a person wasn't loving or didn't add value to our lives or what we were trying to do, then we didn't need him or her in our lives, nor did we have to listen to what he or she had to say. In taking control of our lives we were getting to decide what our value was; we didn't allow it to be determined by anybody else.

We alone can decide what we hold true about ourselves. Nobody has the right to do that for us. Every individual and every family has to decide about their own identity, no matter what gossip or attacks or unkind actions others take.

This is one reason why working on boundaries is very important in the healing process. Having the understanding that you get to decide what you let into your heart, what you let affect you and your self-image, is one of the most important steps in the healing process. It has helped me turn my life around and it has given me the strength to stand up to forces that oppose me without being deeply affected by them.

FINDING A MENTOR

I also believe it is important to align yourself with people that you can learn from—people who want more out of life not only for themselves but for others as well. It is great if you can find someone to talk to who is more experienced than you are and who is further along the road.

When I met Chris Anderson, I knew he was just this type of person. As the Executive Director of MaleSurvivor, Chris is passionate in his pursuit of helping others. After I contacted him, he drove down to see me and we chatted over breakfast. I don't think I spoke much, but I was in awe of how this man, a survivor of child sexual victimization himself, could speak so clearly about what he suffered and the things he had gone on to do. I knew right away Chris was someone that I could look up to as a mentor as I started my own organization, Peaceful Hearts. More importantly, I knew he was someone I could learn from about the healing journey. I have learned many things from Chris and I am grateful that he is always willing to help me when I call upon him.

These are the types of people we need to surround ourselves with, especially as survivors on the path of healing. We need people who will lift us up. Sometimes we need people who will even be able to carry us for a time. We never need people whose intentions are to beat us down. Life is hard enough; don't let other people make it harder. You are in control of what and especially who you let into your life.

GAINING PERSPECTIVE

Life is all about perspective. We must always be mindful of our self-speak or self-talk. If we tell ourselves we are disfigured or that we can't get better, I truly believe that is what we will manifest in our lives.

I remember a commercial that depicted a little boy with a baseball bat and a ball. He said, "I am the best hitter in the world." He threw the ball up, swung, and missed. He picked the ball up, straightened his hat and said again, "I am the best hitter in the world." He threw the ball up again and swung and missed again. He did the same thing one more time. When he threw the ball up the third time, he swung really hard but missed again. He paused and thought for moment then said, "Wow, I'm the greatest pitcher in the world."

That is how we all must start to think. Just because things don't work out the way we think they should doesn't mean we are failures or that there aren't new avenues to try. When we start telling ourselves that we are beautiful, worthy, and powerful, we will start to see beauty, worth, and power showing up in our lives.

We talk about victims and survivors when we discuss child sexual victimization. Certainly children are victimized by perpetrators. Yet we must stop thinking of ourselves as victims. Victims are the ones that things are done to, and their power is taken away. As a survivor, you do not have to allow things to be done to you any more, and you get to be in control of your own power. You are no longer a victim. That was in the past. You are now a survivor. That is a position of strength. Even the terms we apply to such things are important, as they affect our self-image.

This is why you will never hear me say, from this moment forward, "My offender." That simple and often used phrase tends to tie the offender to the victim and even hints at some ownership of the responsibility for the victimization on the part of the victim. Nothing could be further from the truth. All responsibility, guilt, and shame rest squarely on the shoulders of the offender, and there is no reason for any child victim to carry any of that around with them.

Being mindful of your thoughts is one of the greatest things you can do for self-care. Try to avoid dwelling on how unjust it is that things were done to you that shouldn't have been, or how the pain you are feeling isn't your fault and that therefore you shouldn't have to bear it. I'm not saying that those things aren't true. They are. It's just that I have learned that they serve no purpose in my healing process. I cannot control what happened to me in the past. I wanted to focus on what I have control over and that starts with how I speak to myself and the things I tell myself in the here and now.

THE BLESSINGS OF CHILDREN

My children always have been able to give me perspective. My three oldest children were born prematurely; my daughters were both born at less than two and a half pounds. We were told that they could have major health issues in the years to come, but that hopefully they would be okay. Those three children have grown up to be beautiful and healthy. My oldest daughter will start high school in a year, and my other daughter will be in middle school. I have always been amazed by their courage to overcome whatever obstacles were placed in front of them. They are all succeeding in school and have been blessed with good health. When I think that life is unfair or how terrible the things that were done to me were, or when I think of my own pain that was inflicted on me by the actions of another, I look at my kids and see how they are turning out. Not everyone is blessed with healthy, resilient, intelligent, and courageous kids. So I count the blessings as well as the drawbacks of life, and find I am not doing so badly after all.

In February of 2014 my youngest son had a grand mal seizure. He was eighteen months old. It was the scariest thing I have ever experienced. He went limp and I had to perform CPR until the police and ambulance showed up. He was rushed to the hospital and then moved to a more specialized hospital once he was stabilized. His blood sugar was at 20; normal is between 75 and 100. To make a long story short, he had to stay in the hospital for five days; he had to have an IV in his hand, he was pricked every four hours, even when sleeping, to check his blood sugar levels. He had every right to be upset, irritable, and miserable over his situation, but not for one moment was he any of those things. They had to put his IV on a wheeled holder so he could walk around, yet he kept a happy mood and allowed the doctors to do what they needed to do. He would even peek out through the door at the nurses and flirt with them and giggle.

My children have always taught me perspective and shown me courage and resilience in suffering. They, along with my wife Kim, are my inspiration for writing this book. I want them to always know that they can overcome anything. They can always lean on me, as I have leaned on them. I want to thank them for always keeping me grounded.

CREATE YOUR OWN HAPPINESS

I chose to stop focusing on the bad things that happened to me. I knew that if I wanted to heal and reach my dreams, I was the one who was going to have to make that happen. Happiness is something I create, not something I sit around waiting and hoping for.

I started to focus on what a gift and blessing life truly is. How amazing it is to wake up every morning and to see my beautiful wife and kids' faces! I trained my mind to start seeing the positives. I started living in the present and not the past. I started thinking about what I could control and I let go of the rest.

As I sit here writing in this moment, I will not say I'm perfect and completely healed, but I am trying. I believe that is all any of us can do, and that is a lot. Life is still good. There are always new frontiers to conquer. There is joy in the everyday blessings;

we only have to count them to realize that, even if we have suffered a great deal, we have also been given a great deal. I choose to focus on the good and the positive.

Oprah once said that the more you celebrate in your life, the more you will find to celebrate. From one survivor to another, I have to say those are some of the wisest words I have ever heard spoken. I choose to celebrate my life, and in doing so, I find more and more to be grateful for.

Our Inner Child

The final aspect of my journey that I want to speak about is the one I believe has been the most beneficial and most important. It was reconnecting with my child self. A sidebar in the beginning of this book shows a deep experience I had with this profoundly traumatized part of me. I think the reader can sense how very healing that experience was.

The poet Arthur Rimbaud said something very important about recovering your childhood. He said that genius is being able to recover your childhood at will. Well, the genius of healing from child sexual victimization definitely involves recovery of a person's childhood through inner child work. The ability to heal from within is a power that goes beyond each and every one of us as individuals, and yet is within us all. Inner child work taps into this tremendous source of healing.

There are many ways to access the traumatized child self, and for me it was through writing. I wanted this part of myself to know that I did not hold him responsible for what Jerry did to him. I thanked him for being so brave for so many years and for carrying the weight of our secret on his small shoulders for so long. I told him it was now time for him to be a kid again and to be free to grow and change rather than be frozen in time through trauma. Giving him reassurance that, as an adult, I would carry the weight now, I promised him that I would do the hard work to make sure we put the past to rest safely and correctly. I assured him that he would never be hurt again in that way and that he could start to trust. I told him how great it was to have him in my life once again and how happy that made me feel. To see the child I had been and to liberate him from his shell of silence, pain, and fear made me feel whole again. We hugged and I set off to finish this journey.

This was a very hard step to reach and in doing so opened up so much more hurt than I could have imagined. If I had treated my own children the way I was treating my child self all these years, I never would have been allowed to be around kids. I had kept my child self locked up in the prison of my pain and my silence, where he couldn't grow up, where a part of me couldn't grow up and be healed. Until I realized that he needed the nurturing he had never received and that I was the one to do it for him, I was forcing him to remain imprisoned, with guilt and shame as his cellmates. Since taking this step I still write to him and check in. It has helped me tremendously to envision setting him free and letting him be the kind of kid he was meant to be, instead of the poor, undeveloped, frightened person who had so much to hide and so much to fear.

As adult survivors we must realize that the innocent child who was so badly hurt still exists within us all. Part of the healing journey is to help nurture those inner children and allow them to be free to experience life as a child should. We can do this in many ways, and each one is valuable during the journey. We must start to see the world through a child's eyes. As survivors of child sexual victimization, we want the eyes of our inner child, our child self, to be happy, innocent and joyous, the way children should be. We do not want our inner children to be scared and shame-filled. Every child deserves to be happy.

I would urge you to do so when you're ready to take the steps to reconnect with that child. Sit down and have that hard conversation and finally free yourself to live a fulfilled life. Let the bruised and battered child within you out. Comfort him or her. Reassure him or her. Tell the child to grow and change and be free because you, the adult, are in charge now and the child can come out of hiding and enjoy the sunlight of freedom.

You will be comforted deep within your heart and soul as your heal your inner child, as you love the injured and traumatized part of you that was sexually victimized. This child will respond with relief and love as he or she knows there is now a loving adult in charge of your inner existence and they will never have to suffer in that way ever again, because now you are there to protect them, and together you have survived.

This is deep, metaphysical work that takes place in some of the most profound parts of the human psyche. Doing it, you will love yourself as you were meant to be loved, and your inner self will blossom, grow, and sigh in relief, as it is at long last treated with the dignity and care every human being deserves.

It may seem hard. But let's encourage ourselves by remembering these wise words of Nelson Mandela: "It always seems impossible until it's done."

A Final Word

Nobody can predict the twists and turns we will encounter as we move forward in our process, but, as survivors of childhood sex crimes, we can be sure that the journey will be filled with many ups and downs, pain and healing. In doing the hard work to heal, we make our past a blessing instead of a curse, a source of more profound healing than we would undertake had we had more "normal" lives.

As I sit here in this moment I have a completely different outlook on life than I have ever had before. One thing I know for sure is that I survived for a reason bigger than myself. I will continue to share my experiences and advocate for those by sharing my experiences and advocating for those still trying to find their way. I will be a friend and an ally who will go to battle for any survivor who needs help. The healing journey is a difficult one, but I can tell you that the benefits far outweigh the pain in the end. When you can learn to love yourself, fight through the pain, and live a fulfilled life, you will no longer fear the darkness.

What I wish for every survivor is that he or she gets to spread his or her wings and get the opportunity to experience the many wonderful things that life has to offer. We all deserve that. Always know that you are not alone; you are worthy of healing, and healing does happen. Know especially, above and beyond everything else, that you are loved for the precious, priceless, and irreplaceable human being that you are.

Epilogue

The Jerry Sandusky case was a sensational one, causing a huge media frenzy. Many important people lost their jobs over the handling of it, Jerry lost his freedom, and the victims of his crimes gained some closure and vindication for all they had endured at his hands. It is not over either. The filing of lawsuits, counter lawsuits, people coming forward, and new charges continue to this day.

My role in exposing the truth of my past with Jerry re-victimized me in some ways and also affected my family. It has at times given me pause as to how costly disclosure can be. However, since disclosure is the first step in healing from child sexual victimization, it must always be maintained that it is worth doing when and if the person is ready.

My family suffered more upheaval than most victim's families might because of the infamy of the case. At the same time, the very sensationalism of the case can be interpreted to be a blessing in disguise. Because the perpetrator was famous and because I bear his last name, I am able to draw attention to the situation of sexually victimized children and to serve as a catalyst for healing for those who have experienced this awful trauma. I can see that because I was involved in so famous a case, I have more leverage to reach out than the average survivor. I wish to use that fame and leverage to educate the public about child sexual victimization so that we as a society can work to prevent it and to give its victims the resources they need to overcome this most intimate and invasive form of child traumatization.

PEACEFUL HEARTS

Peaceful Hearts is the foundation my wife Kim and I formed to help survivors of child sexual victimization. I'll tell you a little about the genesis of the Foundation's name, because I feel that, more than anything, shows what we are all about.

Peaceful Hearts was a name chosen based on a story I once heard entitled "The Real Meaning of Peace."

The story goes like this . . .

There once was a king who offered a prize to the artist who could paint the best picture of peace. Many artists tried. The king looked at all the pictures. There were only two he really liked, and he had to choose between them.

One picture was of a calm lake. The lake was a perfect mirror for the peaceful, towering mountains all around it. Overhead was a blue sky with fluffy white clouds. All who saw this picture thought that it was a perfect picture of peace.

The other picture had mountains, too, but these were rugged and bare. Above was an angry sky, from which rain fell, and in which lightning played. Down the side of the mountain tumbled a foaming waterfall. This did not look peaceful at all.

But when the king looked closely, he saw behind the waterfall a tiny bush growing in a crack in the rock. In the bush a mother bird had built her nest. There, in the midst of the rush of angry water, sat the mother bird on her nest, in perfect peace.

Which picture do you think won the prize? The king chose the second picture. Do you know why? "Because," explained the king, "peace does not mean to be in a place where there is no noise, trouble or hard work. Peace means to be in the midst of all those things and still be calm in your heart. That is the real meaning of peace."

—*Author Unknown*

Isn't that so true? We all yearn for a peaceful life and wish that every day could be serene, prosperous, and sunny. Yet every day isn't like that. We have to learn to cultivate peace within and to be able to hold on to that inner peace even when the storms of life hit. That is what real peace is.

To us, "Peaceful Hearts" seemed like the perfect name for the kind of organization we wanted to create. Peaceful hearts were certainly what we were searching for in the midst of all the storms we were experiencing. The message would be that every individual has the power within himself or herself to find peace, no matter how the world is swirling around him or her. We think it is important not to let the outside world tell you what peace is; along with your search you get to define what peace is to you. For us it was our home and our children. We turned to each other, and while the storm raged on outside, we were protected because we had love and peace inside our nest.

Through the Peaceful Hearts Foundation, Kim and I have chosen to be advocates and voices for those not yet able to find their own voices. As Peaceful Hearts approaches our first anniversary, we have built a strong foundation.

The one thing we value more than anything is the trust of the survivor community. That is why child sexual victimization survivors are at the forefront of everything we do. This year we hope to launch programs that will aid survivors in finding the help they need and deserve; we will aid in educating the public as a whole on the issue of child sexual victimization; and we will create a safe environment for survivors to come together to share their stories. We want to put a call out to all survivors in the hope that they will answer and that Peaceful Hearts can become the largest community of child sexual victimization survivors working together to heal. We want to create a place where hope and healing are paramount, and where individuals are given the love and respect we all deserve.

Survivors of child sexual victimization are some of the most courageous, loving, compassionate and strong people that I know. At Peaceful Hearts, we want to honor them. We want to lift up survivors as people of strength and courage rather than have them feel as though they are less than or not good enough because of something that happened to them that they had no control over when they were young. Peaceful Hearts wants to help every survivor find his or her power to rise above the victimization and assert his or her intrinsic human value and worthiness.

The only way Peaceful Hearts can succeed is if survivors join our fight. There are approximately 42 million survivors of child sexual victimization in the United States. Eight hundred plus children are sexually victimized in our country each day. Sadly, two out of three will never disclose their sexual victimization to any other human being. This allows perpetrators to work among us unchecked; it also hinders the person's own healing. We want to create a safe forum where they no longer have to hide, where they can find their value, and where they can heal from the trauma. At Peaceful Hearts, we believe every child and survivor of childhood sexual victimization should feel safe, supported, and empowered to thrive.

By raising public awareness through media engagements, community events, informational campaigns, education programs, and legislative action, we seek the elimination of childhood sexual victimization from every community. I travel constantly, going from venue to venue, serving to help people identify the common myths about child sexual victimization and to help them recognize phenomena like grooming, the community "nice guy," and the wall of denial that is put up by both perpetrators and victims.

Child sexual victimization is an insidious part of our society and every society. It is known as a silent epidemic. Because even normal sexual matters have so many taboos attached to them, people don't like to talk or hear about child sexual victimization. It makes us uncomfortable, so it often makes us silent, uneasy, wanting to avoid the issue and the victims' stories. Yet the silence helps perpetrators keep operating. The victims' shame and doubts about letting anyone know what is going on keeps them silent too, serving as unwitting enablers of the child sexual offender. Child sex offenders often know this and manipulate and maneuver their victims into maintaining a code of quiet that is harmful to the victim, other victims and potential victims.

Peaceful Hearts is a safe place to break the silence about child sexual victimization. Victims need to know they are not alone; far from it. Child sexual victimization is common; it is more common than many other dangers we warn children continually about, such as being careful crossing streets so as not to be run over by a car. Many more children are sexually victimized than are run over by cars in our society. Could you possibly imagine a world in which we didn't warn our children about the dangers of crossing the street because we didn't feel comfortable talking about this real and present danger? Yet, because we are uncomfortable talking to our children about sex and sex offenders, we fail to warn them that the greatest risk they face is from people we know and trust and love.

It is important for people to know that there is a large child sexual victimization survivor community ready to embrace and help and to believe the victims' testimony, even if no one else does. We want to build a wall of support around victims and survivors so they have a safe place to be and to share and to know that they are not alone; they are not the only ones; and that they can and will get over child sexual victimization and even come to thrive because of the lessons learned in recovering from it.

We are also here to help raise community awareness so that child sexual victimization can be detected and prevented. The more awareness grows, the more the silence and secrecy will be broken, and the more sunlight can shine in on this widespread social problem that festers in the darkness. Child sexual victimization is the single worst health epidemic that children face. It is probably the least talked about too.

My work requires travel as I go from community to community, raising awareness about child sexual victimization so as to support those who have survived it and alert those who may be in a position to prevent it. Part of raising awareness was to participate in Happy Valley, a documentary by film director Amir Bar-Lev about the Jerry Sandusky scandal at Penn State. The film scans the community surrounding Penn State and sees that an emotional, not to mention a financial, kind of dependency tended to freeze in place the dire need to have taken stronger action against Jerry Sandusky sooner. It shows how frenzied and divided feelings were about Joe Paterno, and how the town reacted.

No community is immune from child sexual victimization, not even, as we have seen, the Eden-like Happy Valley. However, by breaking the silence that walls victimization in, we can all rise like a great phoenix from the ashes. We will create a tomorrow that will allow us all to not only survive but also to thrive—together.

The movie *Happy Valley* ends with footage of me renovating a basement for my children to play in. This is a basement full of light, love, and the happiness and freedom of innocent childhood. Like the basement, this book is part of the legacy that I want to leave for my children. I want them to understand what I went through and that I persevered and came out on top, living life on my terms, and that I have become happy and free. I have always said that if my children know that at the end of my time their dad loved them and was always there to stand up for and fight for them, as I learned to stand up and fight for myself, then I have succeeded. To my wife, my children and to children everywhere, I dedicate this book.

Common Myths
for Perpetrators

Myth: He looks normal and acts normal, so he can't be a child molester.

A common and dangerous public assumption is that a person who looks normal and acts normal simply cannot be a child molester. Sex offenders are knowledgeable about the importance of their public image, and can hide their private behaviors from their friends, neighbors, colleagues, and even their own family members.

Sex offenders use a number of strategies which allow them to gain access to children while hiding their true actions. Many perpetrators seek out volunteer or employment positions that place adults in close proximity to children. Some child molesters appear to be charming, socially responsible, caring, compassionate, morally sound, and sincere. Parents and other responsible adults trust these individuals. This leads to continued access to child victims.

Myth: Only Men Sexually Abuse Children.

While male perpetrators tend to be the majority of reported cases of abuse, women are also capable of child sexual assault. Reports of female perpetrators are on the rise, and female offenders have been reported in cases of abuse involving both male and female children.

Myth: Child molesters target any and all children nearby.

Just because a child is in the proximity of a sex offender, this does not mean that the child will automatically become a target or a victim. This may seem obvious, but some people believe that if a perpetrator didn't abuse a certain child to whom he had nearby, then the children who do make an outcry of abuse must be lying. Sex offenders carefully select and groom their targeted victims, employing an outline or plan to get a particular child alone. Not every child fits the mold of what a pedophile is looking for. There is a process of obtaining a child's friendship or trust, and in some cases, the parent's friendship or trust, as well. Once trust has been obtained, the child is more vulnerable, both emotionally and physically.

MYTH: STRANGER DANGER

93% of all reported cases of child molestation involve a child and a known perpetrator. It is not the stranger in the park carrying out most cases of sexual abuse – it is the people you have in your home. The people most likely to abuse a child are the ones with the most opportunity, most access, and most trust. Abusers can be parents, step-parents, uncles, aunts, step-siblings, babysitters, tutors, and family friends.

MYTH: PEOPLE ARE TOO QUICK TO BELIEVE AN ABUSER IS GUILTY, EVEN IF THERE IS NO SUPPORTING EVIDENCE.

In truth, people are too quick to believe that the accused is innocent, even if there is plenty of supporting evidence. In truth, it is hard for most people to imagine how any person could sexually abuse a child. Because they can't imagine a "normal" person doing such a heinous act, they assume that child molesters must be monsters. If the accused does not fit this stereotype (in other words if he/she appears to be a normal person), then many people will disbelieve the allegation, believing the accused to be incapable of such an act.

MYTH: HUNDREDS OF INNOCENT MEN AND WOMEN HAVE BEEN FALSELY ACCUSED AND SENT TO PRISON FOR MOLESTING CHILDREN.

Over and over again, the media has raised the question whether America is in the midst of a hysterical overreaction to the perceived threat from pedophiles. Actual research, shows that, as a whole, our society continues to under-react and under-estimate the scope of the problem.

Prior to the 1980s, child sexual victimization was largely ignored, both by the law and by society as a whole. In the 1980s, when the scope of the problem began to be acknowledged, the police began to arrest adults accused of child abuse. A backlash quickly formed and police and prosecutors were soon accused of conducting "witch hunts." Although some early cases were handled badly—mainly because the police had little experience in dealing with very young child witnesses—there is little evidence to back the assertion that there was widespread targeting of innocent people.

In fact, research has consistently shown that few abusers are ever identified or incarcerated. Estimates suggest that only 3% of all cases of child sexual victimization and only 12% of rapes involving children are ever reported to police.

RESOURCES:

URL: http://www.leadershipcouncil.org/1/res/csa_myths.html
Article Title: EIGHT COMMON MYTHS ABOUT CHILD SEXUAL VICTIMIZATION

Website Title: The Leadership Council
URL: http://www.onewithcourage.org/wp-content/uploads/2011/09/myths-about-abuse1.pdf

COMMON MYTHS ABOUT VICTIMS OF CHILD SEXUAL VICTIMIZATION

MYTH: ABUSED CHILDREN ALWAYS TELL!

Children often fail to disclose their abuse. This is frequently used as purported evidence that a victim's story isn't plausible. Children who have been victims of sexual assault often have extreme difficulty in disclosing their victimization. One in four girls and one in six boys will be a victim of sexual abuse before his or her 18th birthday, but it is estimated that only one in ten will make an outcry of abuse. It is very common that if a child does make a disclosure, it will not be immediate. Children take time to process, understand what has occurred and realize that they should tell.

A number of factors affect a child's ability to tell his or her story. The age of the child can be a factor, along with a family relationship to the perpetrator, or continuous sexual abuse over a long period of time. Sex offenders will emotionally victimize a child to prevent the truth from being uncovered. A perpetrator can convince a child that the child is to blame him or herself for the bad act. A perpetrator may threaten physical harm to a family member, friend, parent, household pet, or the victim directly. A perpetrator can make a child feel that a disclosure would 'ruin' the family. Boy children may be reluctant to make an outcry because of the social stigma attached to abuse by another male. Children experience fear, embarrassment, guilt, and shame. These feelings are enough to prevent a child from making an allegation of sexual abuse.

MYTH: THE VICTIM IS ALWAYS A GIRL.

Just as women can be sex offenders, boys may be victims of abuse. Unfortunately, child sexual victimization with male victims is underreported due to social and cultural attitudes: boys are taught to fight back and not let others see vulnerability. Boys are aware at an early age of the social stigma attached to sexual assault by another male, and fear appearing weak to others. All of these attitudes make male child victims less likely to tell of their abuse.

MYTH: CHILD VICTIMS OF SEXUAL ABUSE WILL HAVE PHYSICAL SIGNS OF THE ABUSE.

Frequently, an absence of physical evidence is often used as support that a perpetrator must be innocent of an alleged sexual assault. The truth is that abnormal genital findings are rare, even in cases where abuse has been factually proven by other forms of evidence. Many acts leave no physical trace. Injuries resulting from sexual abuse tend to heal very quickly, and many times, exams of child victims do not take place on the same day as the alleged act of abuse.

Myth: Sexual victimization as a child will inevitably result in the child growing up to become a sex offender.

Early childhood sexual victimization does not automatically lead to sexually aggressive behaviors. This is a particularly important fact to understand because a misunderstanding can create a terrible stigma for a child who has been sexually abused. While past sexual victimization can increase the likelihood of sexually aggressive behavior, most children who were sexually victimized never perpetrate against others. Multiple factors contribute to the development of sexually offensive behaviors. These include not only a history of sexual victimization, but also exposure to domestic violence or other violent behaviors.

Myth: Child sexual victimization is a cultural or socioeconomic problem.

It is frequently believed that abuse is a problem plaguing only certain families or people with a certain level of family income and education. Sometimes people believe that incest only happens in lower class and/or rural families. Sexual abuse crosses all socio-economic, neighborhood, race and class barriers. It happens in large and small families; in cities and in rural areas; in wealthy and lower income neighborhoods; and in homes, schools, churches, and businesses.

RESOURCES:

URL: http://www.onewithcourage.org/wp-content/uploads/2011/09/myths-about-abuse1.pdf

RECOMMENDED RESOURCES

Peaceful Hearts Foundation is a 501 c3 nonprofit organization created by Matthew and Kim Sandusky after Matthew disclosed his sexual abuse at the hands of his adopted father, convicted child perpetrator, Jerry Sandusky. Peaceful Hearts provides survivor-informed advocacy for the elimination of childhood sexual victimization and trauma. The organization raises awareness about CSA through media and community events, as well as education and information campaigns that enable the public to proactively participate in creating a community that is free of child abuse and safe for survivors to heal. Peaceful Hearts is committed to developing resources and programs that empower survivors to find their voices and reclaim their lives. They believe there is power and support in bringing survivors together to share their experiences and that its is something that needs to be promoted in all communities.

PEACEFUL HEARTS FOUNDATION

State College, PA 16803
www.peacefulheartsfoundation.org

DARKNESS TO LIGHT

Darkness to Light is a nonprofit organization with a mission to eliminate the incidence and impact of child sexual victimization in order to allow children to grow up healthy and whole. Their program, Stewards of Children, raises awareness of the prevalence and consequences of child sexual victimization by educating adults about the steps they can take to prevent, recognize, and react responsibly to the reality of child sexual victimization. 1064 Gardner Road Suite 210, Charleston, SC 29407, www.d2l.org

MALESURVIVOR

MaleSurvivor provides critical resources to male survivors of sexual trauma and all their partners in recovery by building communities of Hope, Healing, & Support. Since 1994, MaleSurvivor has provided evidence based, trauma informed, and survivor empowering resources healing resources for survivors, professionals, and partners of survivors all across the North America. 4768 Broadway #527, New York, NY 10034 www.malesurvivor.org

LITTLE WARRIORS

Little Warriors is a national, charitable organization based in Canada committed to the awareness, prevention and treatment of child sexual victimization. Little Warriors provides information about the prevalence and frequency of child sexual victimization and healing and support resources. They also offer treatment through the Be Brave Ranch for children between the ages of 8 and 12 who have been sexually abused. PO Box 92507 Sherwood Park, AB T8A 3X4 www.littlewarriors.ca

NATIONAL CHILDREN'S ALLIANCE

National Children's Alliance (NCA) is the national association and accrediting body for Children's Advocacy Centers (CACs). Formed in 1988, NCA has been providing support, technical assistance, and quality assurance for CACs, while serving as a voice for abused children for more than 25 years. A children's advocacy center is a child-friendly facility in which law enforcement, child protection, prosecution, mental health, medical and victim advocacy professionals work together to investigate abuse, help children heal from abuse, and hold offenders accountable. 516 C Street NE, Washington, DC 20002, www.nationalchildrensalliance.org

STOP IT NOW!

Stop It Now! prevents the sexual abuse of children by mobilizing adults, families, and communities to take actions that protect children before they are harmed. They provide support, information, and resources to keep children safe and create healthier communities. Since 1992, they have identified, refined, and shared effective ways for individuals, families, and communities to act to prevent child sexual victimization before children are harmed—and to get help for everyone involved. 351 Pleasant Street, Suite B-319, Northampton, MA 01060, www.stopitnow.org

1IN6'S

1in6's mission focuses on helping adult males who have had unwanted or abusive sexual experiences in childhood to live healthier, happier lives; and to support those who care about them, and professionals providing healing services. PO Box 222033, Santa Clarita, CA 91322, www.1in6.org

NATIONAL CENTER FOR MISSING AND EXPLOITED CHILDREN

National Center for Missing and Exploited Children (NCMEC) opened in 1984 to serve as the nation's clearinghouse on issues related to missing and sexually exploited children. Today NCMEC is authorized by Congress to perform 22 programs and services to assist law enforcement, families and the professionals who serve them. Charles B. Wang International Children's Building, 699 Prince Street, Alexandria, VA 22314, www.missingkids.org

PAVE

PAVE is a nonprofit organization that stands for Promoting Awareness Victim Empowerment. It uses social, educational, and legislative tactics to shatter the silence of sexual abuse. Founder Angela Rose was abducted at knifepoint at age seventeen from the parking lot of the mall where she worked and was assaulted by a repeat sex offender on parole for murder. Instead of staying silent, Angela took a stand and worked with survivors as well as the community to help enact Illinois's Sexual Dangerous Persons Commitment Act in 1998. 233 S. Wacker Dr. 84th Floor, Chicago, IL 60606 www.pavingtheway.net

VOICEFOUND

Voicefound was founded in 2011, Voice Found is a Canadian non-profit organization that is committed to preventing Child sexual victimization and proactively supporting the healing and recovery of individuals and communities from the health, financial and emotional impacts of that abuse. www.voicefound.ca

RAPE, ABUSE, AND INCEST NATIONAL NETWORK (RAINN)

Rape, Abuse, and Incest National Network (RAINN) is the nation's largest antisexual assault organization. RAINN operates the National Sexual Assault Hotline, Online Hotline, and confidential services; educates the public about sexual assault; and leads national efforts to prevent sexual assault, improving services to survivors and ensuring that rapists are brought to justice. 1220 L Street, NW, Suite 505, Washington, DC 20005 www.rainn.org

Safe 4 Athletes

Safe 4 Athletes is a not-for-profit organization that:

Advocates for and helps sports organizations adopt effective policies, procedures and educational programs that are designed to prevent coach, volunteer and peer misconduct whether it be abuse (sexual, verbal, emotional or physical) bullying, harassment or other forms of inappropriate behaviors.

Assists sports organizations faced with situations involving sexual misconduct, bullying, harassment and other forms of inappropriate conduct on how to handle these situations appropriately and act quickly to restore safe environments for athletes.

Provides a safe and confidential place where abused athletes, their parents or others concerned about the impact of coach/volunteer/peer misconduct can call

Encourages and helps educate all parents and athletes to be more aware of what they can do to recognize inappropriate coach/volunteer/peer behavior and understand how traumatic the effects of such experiences can be for athletes.

Partners with state, regional, and national sports governing associations and other national sports organizations to encourage the adoption of legislation mandating that their members adopt strong policies, procedures and educational programs regarding this issue. PO Box 650, Santa Monica, CA 90406 www.safe4athletes.org

Made in the USA
San Bernardino, CA
20 April 2016